MY EYES HAVE SEEN

MY HANDS HAVE TOUCHED

MY TONGUE HAS TASTED

THE KINGDOM OF HEAVEN

*My Eyes Have Seen My Hands Have Touched
My Tongue Has Tasted The Kingdom Of Heaven*

Copyright © 2023 Richard G. Manning M.D.. All rights reserved.

No rights claimed for public domain material, all rights reserved. No parts of this publication may be reproduced, stored in any retrieval system, or transmitted in any form or by any means, electronic, mechanical, recording, or otherwise, without the prior written permission of the author. Violations may be subject to civil or criminal penalties.

ISBN: 978-1-63308-725-5 (paperback)
        978-1-63308-726-2 (ebook)

Cover and Interior Design by *R'tor John D. Maghuyop*

PO Box 1665, Rolla MO 65402

Printed in United States of America

MY EYES HAVE SEEN
MY HANDS HAVE TOUCHED
MY TONGUE HAS TASTED
THE KINGDOM OF HEAVEN

Finding Jesus Christ
Hidden in the Sacraments
Between the Beatitudes
And the Lord's Prayer

Richard G. Manning M.D.

Table of Contents

Dedication 7

Prelude 8

I Lost Jesus in the Church Parking Lot 9

Finding Jesus Christ in the Sermon on the
    Mount and the Sacraments 18

Finding Jesus in My Baptism as a Patient..........................22

Finding Jesus in Confession as a Prisoner.........................28

Finding Jesus in My Confirmation as a Manual Laborer 33

Finding Jesus in Holy Communion while Practicing
    Surgery as a Christian in an Islamic Republic......................36

Finding Jesus in Holy Matrimony While Unemployed.....................40

An Exegesis – Parts One through Five of Nine.................44

Finding Jesus in the Anointing of a
    Sick Contemplative Path Builder..49

Finding Jesus in Wounded Healers in the
    Office of Holy Orders 56

Finding Jesus in the Sacramental Economy as a Child
    of the Beatitudes and the Lord's Prayer....................................61

Finding Jesus by Suffering Joyfully Through, In,
    and With Him 66

Continuing the Exegesis – Parts Six and Seven....................69

Pausing to Reflect on Sevens Before Considering
    Eights and Nines..74

Returning to Mass to Complete the Exegesis
 – Parts Eight and Nine 78
Returning to the Church Parking Lot 85
After the Event 89
Searching for Jesus 91
Where Will We Look For Jesus? 94
Finding Jesus 97
The Three Side-by-Side 99
Sermon on the Mount Crossverse Puzzle - version 2 101
References 102

Dedication

To my wife
my co-laborer and prayer warrior

Prelude

"Who is this that comes forth like the dawn,
beautiful as the white moon,
pure as the blazing sun,
fearsome as celestial visions?"

Song of Songs 6:10

I Lost Jesus in the Church Parking Lot

August 7, 2023, approximately 7 am

Holy Name of Jesus Church Parking lot

Have you ever lost Jesus in the church parking lot? You know what I am talking about. It happens far too often, sadly. We leave the church, our faith invigorated, having heard scripture tailor-made for us, ready to preach the gospel, and thirty seconds later, we argue with our wife or someone else over a trivial matter. Worse still, we could end the argument by admitting our mistake, but we're too proud to do that.

I want to tell you a story of another way I lost Jesus in the church parking lot that not's so common, happily. I am a retired general surgeon. For thirty years, I practiced a healing art focused almost entirely on what I could see, feel, and sometimes smell in my own hands. What I received from my senses constituted the concrete reality of today's problem. While exploring an abdomen to diagnose the cause of a small bowel obstruction, a heavy fetid odor indicated the extent of the problem; some part of the bowel had died, and the glistening white irregularly shaped puckering mass on the surface of the cecum and its palpable hard fixation to the retroperitoneum answered why the patient had an obstruction. It told me I had to perform a right hemicolectomy to offer hope for survival.

In other instances, I had to rely almost entirely on my sense of touch, such as when performing a splenectomy. To mobilize a spleen, hidden from view high in the left upper quadrant of the abdomen, protected by the ribs, under the left diaphragm, behind the stomach, to the left of the tail of the pancreas, and above the left kidney and adrenal gland, I was trained to use my fingers to explore and visualize in my mind's eye the many ligamentous attachments which had to be cut sharply and the pulsating vascular bundle which should not be cut until it had been encircled and ligated.

It's been about a decade since I last explored an abdomen. However, I am still using the same concrete senses to navigate through my daily problems and, as it turned out on this day, to navigate to my daily bread on another concrete surface. Let me tell you the story.

At approximately 7 a.m. on Monday, August 7, 2023, I walked out of the small chapel of Holy Name of Jesus Church and joined seven men who had also attended the daily 6:30 Mass. One of the men told us about the results of his cataract surgery one week earlier. "I feel like I have the eyes of a young man," he said. We chatted for a few more minutes, and I then followed one of the men toward the parking lot. We were conversing for a few seconds when I suddenly and accidentally spit a small remaining fragment of the Eucharist out of my mouth. I had no doubts about what had happened. I saw a white piece of the host sail out of my mouth, the same one I had felt a moment before on my tongue. I immediately told my friend. Knowing the event's significance, we stopped dead in our tracks and started looking for it. Without moving my feet, I squatted on my haunches and started exploring the ground with my ten fingertips while searching with my two eyes. Two other men soon joined us. The four of us stared at and digitally explored what I estimate to have been a five-by-seven-foot patch of black asphalt in search of what we knew to be our Lord Jesus Christ, his body, blood, soul, humanity, and divinity.

Finding a small white fragment of anything might have been easy if the backdrop was solid black. Such was not the case here. The asphalt on which the host fell contained innumerable two-to-twenty millimeter-sized yellowish, white, and gray pebbles of variable shapes, all embedded in the black tarry substrate that held them together. Trying to visually distinguish the small piece of host within this variegated mosaic was impossible. Imagine looking at a 1000-piece jigsaw puzzle displaying a picture of ten thousand multi-colored pebbles on a beach and being asked to find one special pebble. Imagine looking at a jar filled with ten thousand multi-colored marbles and being asked to find one special marble. Or, look at the pictures of that same asphalt on the next three pages of this book.

Picture 1 Standing

Picture 2 Stooping

Picture 3 Squatting

I am sorry. I suspect it's boring to look at three successive pictures of a black asphalt parking lot. I didn't know of a better way to convey the magnitude of the problem that confronted us. I will help you find one white pebble to illustrate the point. Look at Picture 3, which I took while squatting. Do you see the yellowish-orange arrowhead about an inch and a half up and over to the left from the lower right corner? If you aren't sure which yellowish-orange arrowhead I am talking about in the black and white picture, look at the front cover of this book. You will see it just to the right of and between the words Beatitudes and Lord's prayer. Follow the tip of the arrow, pointing towards the upper left corner of the picture for less than half an inch, and you'll see the white pebble I want you to find. Now, find that same pebble in the other two pictures. You can find it in both if you are clever and use other landmarks.

Now, if you have found it, I want you to imagine standing, stooping, or squatting over a five-by-seven-foot patch of this asphalt, perhaps the size of a small bathroom floor, and finding a different white pebble about which I offer no clues other than to say it is of a similar shape and size to the one I instructed you to find.

Have you appreciated the magnitude of the problem? Certainly, with our four sets of aged eyes, it would take us a lot of time to find that itty-bitty Eucharist, possibly hours, time we didn't have on a Monday morning at the beginning of a work week. And then, of course, there was the motivation problem. It wasn't that we didn't care. We did care very much. It was that we felt hopeless. The effort felt futile. The idea of finding the host was bewildering, and time was not on our side.

After searching for about ten minutes, we gave up. I went to my car, pondering if I should immediately see Father Quinlan to ask his advice and pardon. I knew I had not sinned mortally. I had no intention of spitting the Eucharistic particle from my mouth. But then, I recalled how I often felt a Eucharistic particle on my tongue while engaged in the bad manners of talking with my mouth full, and I asked myself, could I have acted with more care?

And then, I recalled the scripture readings from Mass that morning and asked myself, could I have paid more attention to the words? It was as if God had whispered to those who organized the readings many years ago, 'Use Lectionary 407 today. Someone who needs another reminder to revere my Word will be in Mass.' I have provided parts of the readings below.

The Old Testament reading: *"The children of Israel lamented, 'Would that we had meat for food! We remember the fish we used to eat without cost in Egypt, and the cucumbers, the melons, the leeks, the onions, and the garlic. But now we are famished; we see nothing before us but this manna. (Nm 11:4b-6)*

The Psalm: *"Those who hated the LORD would seek to flatter me, but their fate would endure forever, While Israel I would feed with the best of wheat, and with honey from the rock I would fill them." (Ps 81:16-17)*

The Gospel acclamation: *One does not live on bread alone, but on every word that comes forth from the mouth of God. (Mat. 4:4)*

The Gospel: *Taking the five loaves and the two fish, and looking up to heaven, he said the blessing, broke the loaves, and gave them to the disciples, who in turn gave them to the crowds. They all ate and were satisfied, and they picked up the fragments left over—twelve* *wicker baskets full. Those who ate were about five thousand men, not counting women and children. (Mat. 14:13-21)*

Talk about a God-given message tailor-made for me. I'm not kidding -those were the words I heard just a few minutes before spitting the Word made flesh out of my mouth. I provided a link at the back of this book to the Catholic Church's Mass readings so you can confirm these were that day's readings. [1]

The sad irony of the morning grew. Was I like the grumbling children of Israel, not appreciating what the Lord provides, not appreciating He who provides the best wheat, miraculously feeds His Church with his Word, and gives her the bread by which she can live forever?

I got into my car and drove a few miles to the hardware store, spoke to several sales clerks, and then dropped off an empty propane tank. Fifteen minutes later, with the words of scripture still swirling in my mind, I drove out of the store's parking lot, and when I came to the first intersection requiring a choice: turn right, go home, and forget the incident, or turn left, drive to the church, and figure out what to do, I turned left.

Finding Jesus Christ in the Sermon on the Mount and the Sacraments

I must provide more context before continuing the story of the search. I have spent the last decade contemplating the Sermon on the Mount after memorizing it and the four chapters in Matthew's gospel that precede it in the first three months of 2014. Additionally, I had spent the three days prior to Monday morning's disaster at a Catholic men's retreat, the theme of which was *A Roadmap for Better Living: A Fresh Look at the Beatitudes*. Ironically, the retreat was hosted by **Corpus Christi** Roman Catholic Church of Chambersburg, Pennsylvania (emphasis mine) at Saint Mary's College in Maryland. With a group of three hundred men, I listened to five compelling talks on the Beatitudes, the first nine sentences of the Sermon on the Mount, participated in a Eucharistic procession, spent several hours in front of the Blessed Sacrament in adoration, and washed my soul in the living water provided by Jesus through the sacraments.

It was my first visit to the college campus. I marveled at the picturesque surrounding landscape and the works of art abundantly scattered about the campus inside and outside its buildings. The weather was perfectly serene, not too hot and breezy at times. The only glitch, if I dare to call it that, was the ten-minute hard downpour of rain which soaked our procession as we moved the protected Eucharistic monstrance from the Immaculate Conception Chapel to Saint Bernard's Chapel in the seminary. To top it all off, I took three contemplative hikes up to the National Shrine Grotto of Our Lady of Lourdes, where more natural and manmade pictures, statues, and mosaics saturated my dry and thirsting soul.

At the end of the weekend, filled with Jesus' presence in nature, art, and especially the Blessed Sacrament, I was "walking on clouds," as they say. My cloud walking was enhanced by the retreat master, Monsignor King. His insights deepened my understanding of the Beatitudes, as did his teaching manner. Poking fun, most commonly at himself, he taught humility, being poor in spirit, by his example just as effectively as he did when unpacking the meaning of the Beatitudes.

At the end of the second day of the retreat, I gave him a copy of a small book I had recently written and published. The book's title is *Beatitudes - Front, Lord's Prayer - Center of the Sermon on the Mount Contemplating Jesus' Call to Suffer Joyfully, A Primer*. Since publishing it about a month before, I had felt reluctant to share it broadly. I wondered if the central theme of my little 45-page booklet was real or more a figment of an overactive imagination. Was I reading too much into the text, projecting a sacramental bias where it had no place?

On the third day after his last presentation, I asked the Monsignor if he would listen to a short imaginary conversation about this *"Primer"* I wanted to have in his presence. I know that sounds funny, but bear with me. He agreed. After the first three parts of the imaginary conversation, he said, 'I like where this is going.' When I finished the imaginary conversation, he smiled and said, 'I think you are on to something. I think it will be very helpful for you to share this booklet more broadly.' I was thrilled and determined to do that and to continue the contemplation and writing that produced the small book I had given him.

I want to clarify something. I don't know how much or even if Monsignor King had read the *"Primer."* In the ten minutes we had between his last talk on the Beatitudes and the Mass he would officiate, and I would attend in twenty minutes at the Church of Saint Mary in front of the Grotto, we didn't talk about the little booklet itself. However, I know he read my bio on the back cover because he told me he had also attended Jefferson Medical College for a year. I assume he also read the short summary of the booklet immediately before my bio. It says this:

"The author hopes this small 'Primer' will stimulate deep contemplation of two of Christianity's most famous and powerful sayings within the context of where Jesus spoke them, chapters five, six, and seven from the Gospel of Matthew, the Sermon on the Mount. Having imbibed the spiritual truths from this starting point of Jesus's teaching ministry, the reader will then follow where Jesus leads to nine mountain-top experiences subtly and not so subtly embedded by Matthew within his gospel to contemplate nine biblical characters, Adam, Abel, Noah, Abraham, Joseph, Moses, (think of Moses and Elijah with Jesus during His transfiguration), David, John the Baptist and Jesus. Lastly, the reader will contemplate the Catholic Church's sacraments as the source of strength Christ gives those traveling the arduous beatific journey away from self-indulgence towards self-giving.)

I want to replay now the imaginary conversation I had with Monsignor King, including many more details than I had time to share with him then. I will provide more personal history, especially innumerable conversations with Jesus Christ focused primarily on His Sermon on the Mount. In this book, I have divided the conversation into nine parts. The conversation started in earnest on June 3, 2002, one day after my forty-fifth birthday and one day after my surgical career took a sharp turn in a new direction. All nine parts of the conversation occurred in nine distinct situations in which God had placed me. I memorized the Sermon on the Mount in 2014 after the fourth of the nine life experiences immediately after I returned home from Afghanistan.

After a protracted time denying God's call on my life, I traveled to Afghanistan, knowing without a doubt that I belonged there. Indeed, a wise and merciful God took a failing and drifting son and stuck him in nine distinct life experiences, orchestrating everything to teach him to appreciate the Beatitudes, the Lord's Prayer, and the sacraments. That same Lord will continue teaching me to live the eighth Beatitude, the one about suffering for as long as I live, teaching me not just through His spoken and subsequently inscripturated words but also through and by living within me as The Lord who took on flesh over two thousand years ago and who now gives Himself to me as often as I attend Mass at a Catholic Church. Let's meet Him now.

Finding Jesus in My Baptism as a Patient

August 2, 2002 – September 20, 2002

The residential treatment center, Argyle, Texas

Imagine looking up at a man in a Catholic Church. You are ten days old. A few minutes before, you had felt him tracing a cross on your forehead and then your chest. Now, you feel water being poured over your head, once, twice, a third time, and hear words- *"I baptize you in the name of the Father and the Son and the Holy Spirit."* You look up, see Jesus, and hear Him say, *"Blessed are the poor in spirit!"*

You are filled with the Holy Spirit and cry out in the gurgling babble of a baby, but God hears, *"Our Father who art in heaven!"*

Jesus responds, and even though you are a newborn, you can hear and understand Him at a deep, visceral level because He has just taken a special place in your heart, mind, and soul. 'My dear friend, how perceptive of you to see my Father when you see me. What great faith you have! You are surely a baptized child of God with whom My Father is well pleased. Otherwise, you surely could not have seen God the Father in my face. You are among those about whom we say, *"For theirs is the kingdom of heaven!"*

Imagine yourself contemplating this scene many years later. Only, this time, after hearing Jesus' promise about your faith, you respond, 'Lord, it hasn't always been this way since my baptism as an infant. Can I talk to you about that?'

Jesus responds, 'I know. I know about the terrible car accident your family suffered when you were four years old. I know how you felt somehow responsible for that accident that could have killed everyone and how you internalized your shame. I know this shame remained deeply embedded in your soul, negatively influencing, at some level, everything you thought, felt, said, and did for the next forty-one years. For this reason, I sent you to a residential treatment center to help you expel those damning feelings Satan has used against you at every opportunity. Cooperate with the therapists, and I will be with you the whole time.'

You and Jesus rehash this special time when you were the patient, not the doctor. 'Lord, on the first morning after my arrival, I took a walk before the breakfast hall opened and the day's events started. I asked God some questions. 'Who am I, Lord? I have lost my medical license and possibly my surgical career. I won't be living with my wife and children for the next year, possibly ten. What does that leave of me as a person if I am not acting as a surgeon, husband, or father? Who am I at the deepest core of my being?'

'Yes, dear friend. I told you to have patience, to be a patient, to experience life for fifty days as a patient, and a very sick one at that. Your therapists and counselors, I told you, will control your schedule, filling it with individual and group sessions, reading, journaling, and sharing your life with them and the other thirty or so patients there, who would also share their stories with you and the rest of the group.'

'Lord, approximately forty days later, I underwent a special therapy session in which one of my therapists guided me through a mental exercise called Eye Movement Desensitization and Reprocessing (EMDR). He told me that EMDR is a form of psychotherapy in which the patient recalls distressing images while the therapist generates bilateral sensory input, such as side-to-side eye movements or tapping. The therapist guided me back to the family car accident in June 1961. It felt so real.

I vividly remember the whole family was together, driving home on a rainy night. I was the only one awake, other than my mother, doing the driving. Oblivious to the danger of driving on bald tires at night during a torrential storm, I jumped around in the back seat, being a nuisance to my mother. Mom repeatedly told me to settle down. Finally, fed up with my shenanigans, she looked around to scold me and, in so doing, lost control of the car. The car swerved, skidded across the road, and collided with another oncoming vehicle. Three of the car's eight passengers, including me, were thrown from the car. I suddenly found myself in a dark, strange, prickly place. Leaves and sticks were pressing against my face. I heard a commotion, crying, and eventually sirens. I felt deeply ashamed in those bushes, knowing something awful had happened, and I felt sure it was my fault. Several minutes passed. I could hear my parents and siblings' familiar voices, but no one came to rescue me. I thought, 'Perhaps I deserve to be left alone to die.' Finally, someone noticed two sneakers sticking out of a bush and kicking like mad and rescued me.'

'My dear friend,' Jesus said with tears in His eyes, 'In your EMDR session, you had the opportunity to relive those events for the first time in over forty years and to confront feelings that had remained tucked away deep inside your psyche, disrupting the well-ordered psyche we had first given you at the moment of your Baptism, tragically disrupting your ability to trust me, tragically disrupting the intimacy we had at first sight. The therapist gently reminded you that you were not responsible for the accident and had no reason to be ashamed.'

'Lord, when I realized this, I felt the weight of shame lifted from my soul. Then, approximately one week after the EMDR session, I underwent another special group therapy session in which one of the counselors guided us through a semi-hypnotic session and led us on a journey into our sub-conscience by asking us to visualize various images. I closed my eyes and cleared my mind. As she narrated, I felt a gentle breeze on my face, listened to the soft murmur of a running brook, and admired many beautiful flowers in an expansive field around me. I was in a very calm and peaceful place. At the therapist's prompting, I walked along a path to the center of a beautiful grove of trees. She told us to envision a bag in our hands and to throw into it all the lies, misconceptions, and negative emotions that had controlled us for many years. I threw shame, fear of abandonment, and others into that bag and then threw the bag away as instructed. Then, something else happened, but it didn't follow the therapist's narrative. She had not suggested anyone else enter this serene environment, but someone did in my case.'

'Yes, my dear friend. I did that. As I watched you sitting in the middle of that peaceful grove, now free of the negative emotions that had bound you for years, I nudged a little boy hiding behind some bushes.'

'And I, Lord, heard a gentle rustling and looked over at the bushes on my right. Was it the Holy Spirit?'

'Whereupon, you saw a small boy, about four years old, emerging with a smile on his face. It was a part of you kept hidden for all those years since the accident, and when he emerged, you recognized him instantly, for you saw too the eyes of God, my eyes, looking back at you.'

'Yes, Lord, as I looked at the boy, I beheld the same eyes I saw at my Baptism and smiled back.'

'Then we held hands and walked out of the garden just as the therapist brought the group back to the surface of consciousness, with you/me free from shame, fear, and guilt for the first time in thirty-seven years,' Jesus and I said in perfect unison. It wasn't the first time we finished sentences for each other.

'Imagine that, Lord. You guided my therapist to expel a demon of shame in just fifty days. I left the center five days later.'

'And on the way home, I shouted into your ear, *"Blessed are the poor in spirit!"*

'And I responded, Thank you, Lord. I understand why you removed me from my proud perch as a successful surgeon, husband, and father and placed me in the humbling situation of being a patient, like a child, dependent on others and you. You wanted to teach me that I am, first and foremost, a beloved child of God. You taught me to appreciate my Baptism and that humility is the starting point to heaven for all of God's children.'

'My dear friend, I asked you if you wanted to say anything else.

'And I, filled with the Holy Spirit, cried out as an adult Catholic who now understands the significance of his Baptism, *"Our Father in heaven!"*

'My dear child, how perceptive of you to see my Father when you see me. What great faith you have! You are surely a baptized child of God with whom My Father is well pleased. Otherwise, you surely could not have seen the family resemblance, could not have seen God the Father in My face. You are among those about whom we say, *"Blessed are the poor in spirit, for theirs is the kingdom of heaven!"*

Finding Jesus in Confession as a Prisoner

September 23, 2002 – July 11, 2003

Cumberland County Prison

Imagine you are ten years old, walking into the confessional in a Catholic Church. You are filled with contrition because you have willfully disobeyed your parents, sinned against God, and received a just punishment. You pour out your soul, expressing your sorrow, and then you hear the priest say, "I absolve you from your sins in the name of the Father and of the Son and of the Holy Spirit." You look up and see Jesus again, looking at you with a big smile, and hear Him say, *"Blessed are they who mourn!"*

You are filled with the Holy Spirit and say, *"Hallowed be your name!"*

Jesus responds, 'My dear friend, how grateful I am that you have returned to reconcile our relationship. I missed you terribly. Please never leave me again, but if you slip one day, and you will, please hurry back to meet me again right here. I'll be waiting. You came in lamenting your sin and for that reason, *"You shall be comforted!"*

Imagine yourself contemplating this scene many years later. Only, this time, after hearing Jesus' comforting words, you respond, 'Lord, why do I keep doing what I know I should not do and not do the things I know I should do?' Can I talk to you about this?'

Jesus responds, 'I know. You have failed many times to live up to the firm amendment to change your life after confessing your sins, which is why I had to send you to prison to learn the ways of the truly penitent.'

'Yes, Lord, I entered prison shortly after leaving the treatment center and again found myself in a situation where I had no responsibilities, no patients to care for, and no children or wife to take responsibility for. However, in contrast to the event-packed days in the treatment center, the only thing on my daily schedule was to be present twice a day at roll call, standing in front of my cell while the guards inspected it.'

'You could have wasted the time. Instead, you spent it learning a new healing art, listening empathetically to other's problems.'

'Yes, Lord. My cell block was full of hurting men. They called me 'doc,' but I had nothing to offer besides an open ear and an understanding word.'

'And yet,' Jesus said, 'you learned how effective empathetic listening can be. Far different than opening and exploring abdomens, you opened souls for me to explore with those willing to meet me there.'

'Yes, Lord, I am aware of your operating skills. *"Indeed, the word of God is living and effective, sharper than any two-edged sword, penetrating even between soul and spirit, joints and marrow, and able to discern reflections and thoughts of the heart." (Heb. 4:12)*

'Near the end of your prison time, you asked God another question about your home life.'

'Yes, Lord, I said, 'Father, given that I am your baptized child, what do you want me to do, and how am I supposed to do it without a medical license? That license was my ticket to an occupation. It qualified me to practice the art."

'It was a great question, and my Father provided another clear answer. He said you are uniquely qualified to love your wife and children. Start there.'

My dear reader, I want to pause here to clarify something. I am not claiming giftedness unique to me. I was and am well aware of my many faults as a husband and father. The giftedness to which I refer is the same that God gives all humanity, all men, women, husbands, wives, fathers, and mothers - the ability to empathize and feel what others are feeling. On top of that, God gives every baptized person three other supernatural gifts to use when answering empathy's call: faith, hope, and love instilled at baptism.

With these gifts, God prompts humanity to want to do something good for the suffering person with whom they empathize and enables them to do it in the right way for the right reasons. In short, He calls and equips humanity to be children made in the image and likeness of God who imitate God by loving all people, especially those closest to them. Unfortunately, save for a relatively small group of loving people, human history tells a different story of hatred, cruelty, indifference, and injustice, including my life. Let's pick up the conversation where we left off.

'Lord, I then reminded you, as if you ever needed reminding, that you knew I wanted to change but couldn't. You knew I had been trying to change for over thirty-five years, that the bad thoughts had led to bad actions- that the bad actions became bad habits, that the bad habits became addictive.'

'And I reminded you, my dear friend, that you meant to say that you couldn't change on your own. However, you could have changed with God's help. All you had to do was cooperate with Him and take advantage of the many graces He puts in front of you, starting with the sacrament of Confession.'

'Yes, Lord, I got to the confessional several times during the interval between the treatment center and prison. Not only that, but my ten months of imprisonment constituted one long confession, obviously not in the Church's confessional but in my moment-by-moment routines. Many nights, I lay in my cell feeling sad, lamenting how I had hurt others. I also felt a lot of pain from the forced separation from my family. I had ignored the dictates of my conscience on occasions far too numerous to count. I resolved to live with integrity, to be inside what I projected to the world outside.'

'My Father, the Holy Spirit, and I could have counted the number of times you ignored us, blatantly disobeyed us, grievously hurting your loved ones and your patients, and us, but we did not. We never count the sins of a person who enters the confessional with a contrite spirit. We are concerned with how they feel when they come home. Do you recall feeling anything else in prison?'

'I do, Lord. Interestingly, I was not feeling shame, guilt, or even fear. Yes, I felt sadness and pain, but joy was my predominant feeling within just a week of entering prison. I realize that may sound odd, but I think it resulted from the renewed faith, hope, and love I felt at the deepest core of my soul. You had revived my soul with your presence, like a cold, fresh splash of water through the baptism of being a patient. Thinking of temperatures, I believe the odd mixture of feelings must resemble what imperfect humans who died striving for union with God feel in purgatory. Still encumbered with many character flaws when they die, they experience the pain of letting go of what they should not love and the joy of knowing God is drawing them closer to Him. Not only this, but I am certain I felt great relief. For the first time in a very long time, I was not shackled with the burden of living a lie. The truth was out. The law bound my hands with cuffs and shackled my feet, but you, Lord, unshackled my soul from that grievous burden of living a double life.'

'My dear friend, when a prodigal son returns home, we feel nothing but pure joy.'

I answered with tears in my eyes. 'Lord, every time I return to mourn my sins in the sacrament of Penance, to reconcile our relationship, I find a loving Father, anxious to forgive me, just like the prodigal son. Every time you receive me back, I feel joy. What else can I pray at those moments but *"Hallowed be thy name?"*

'Indeed, to those who genuinely mourn their sins, we say, *"Blessed are they who mourn, for they shall be comforted."*

Finding Jesus in My Confirmation as a Manual Laborer

July 15, 2003 – December 25, 2004

Building Homes, Harrisburg, Pennsylvania

Imagine yourself in the Catholic Church again, about ten days after your first confession. You feel the bishop anointing your forehead with holy chrism and hear him say, "Be sealed with the Gift of the Holy Spirit." You see Jesus again with a big smile and hear Him say, *"Blessed are the meek!"*

You are filled with the Holy Spirit and respond, *"Thy kingdom come, thy will be done, on earth as it is in heaven!"*

Jesus answers, 'My dear soldier, how courageous you are. You could never have known nor desired my will to be done on earth as it is in heaven in your life unless you had first received the sacrament of Confirmation, which unites you more perfectly to the Church and enriches you with the supernatural gifts of the Holy Spirit. You are fully equipped to embark on your life's journey, a newly empowered soldier of God, to proclaim the gospel in word and deed without fear. To you and your blessed comrades in arms, the Church militant on earth, I say, *"You shall inherit the earth!"*

You respond, 'Lord, it hasn't always been this way with me since my Confirmation. Can I talk to you about that?'

Jesus responds, 'I know. You have often failed to proclaim the gospel, but there will be a time for you to do that again. For this reason, I arranged a situation for you upon your release from prison in which you will learn true meekness. Let me clarify, - meekness is not weakness. Meekness is strength through reliance on God instead of self, learning to ask God for help rather than pushing ahead with unaided, unqualified, blind self-confidence. You must learn to cultivate meekness through prayer. Prayer is to the soldier of Christ what the shovel is the battalion soldier digging in to prepare for the enemy's assault. Learn to use the shovel of prayer often and effectively.'

'Yes, Lord, immediately after my release from prison, I started working for a home-building company where my hands used a putty knife and paintbrush to finish homes instead of pickups and a needle holder to finish operations. The company paid me far less for this manual labor than what I was paid as a surgeon.'

'Of course, my friend, but God placed much more value on it because you were cooperating with His graces and praying. You started living with integrity. The surgeon was subdued but very much depending on God.'

'Lord,' I responded with tears in my eyes, 'I built homes with a humble group of blue-collar workers learning simple but profound life lessons such as the value of humility. I further refined the art of listening to others attentively, especially those I once thought were beneath me because of their lack of education. Ironically, I, the educated one, offered little knowledge to my coworkers, but they didn't hold that against me. Rather, they modeled patience by teaching me one new skill after the next. I learned the value of not taking life too seriously, in the sense that the resolution of problems did not depend on me, the self-exalted one, to fix, but rather on the loving actions of God, who even works through mere humans like me, the greatest of sinners.'

'Yes, my dear friend, as your awareness of your sinful nature increased, you learned to respect all men and women without passing judgment on them. Not only this, but through these three life experiences, fifty days as a baptized patient, ten months as a confessing prisoner, and two years as a confirmed laborer, God reinforced the sacramental graces started in your youth. The timing could not have been better. God had to prepare you for your next experience, a nine-year assignment in Kabul, Afghanistan.'

'Lord, I marvel at God's provision and timing.'

'My dear friend, God is a master builder. He lays the foundation in Baptism, which he strengthens in Confirmation and sustains through Confession. Additionally, by opening your mind to the truths of the first three Beatitudes and your heart to the first three parts of my Prayer, God solidified these three sacraments in you as an adult.'

'Yes, I am thankful He did that, and I mean it when I pray, *"Thy kingdom come, thy will be done on earth as it is in heaven."*

You learned Godly meekness, and you have prayed the exact words I have given to continue growing in that meekness, so I repeat, although there is no reason on my part to repeat anything, for I always mean what I say, *"Blessed are the meek, for they shall inherit the earth."*

Finding Jesus in Holy Communion while Practicing Surgery as a Christian in an Islamic Republic

October 13, 2004 – November 17, 2013

Working with CURE International in Afghanistan

Imagine thirty-five years after your Confirmation; you are standing with other Catholics at Mass in the Italian Embassy in Kabul, Afghanistan. You watch the priest stretch his hands over the bread and chalice of wine and hear him say, "Be pleased, O God, we pray, to bless, acknowledge, and approve this offering in every respect; make it spiritual and acceptable, so that it may become for us the Body and Blood of your most beloved Son, our Lord Jesus Christ."

Jesus speaks, and you hear, *"Blessed are they who hunger and thirst for righteousness!"*

With the others, you pray, *"Give us this day our daily bread!"*

A bit later in the liturgy, you walk to the altar and hear the priest say, "The Body of Christ." You see Jesus and hear him say passionately, 'My dear friend, how loving you are. You are ready to receive me in the Eucharist with a deep and abiding faith. You shall receive all of me, body, soul, humanity, and divinity. Keep receiving me in Holy Communion, for surely, *"You shall be satisfied!"*

You respond, 'Lord, it hasn't always been this way with me. Can I talk to you about that?'

'My dear friend, I know how often you have denied the love I have offered to you in Holy Communion, how often you have not thanked me in your actions after receiving me in the Eucharist, how often you have tried to find fulfillment by yielding to your disordered appetite instead of being satisfied with the bread of life I give you. To ensure that you never again take the love I offer you in Holy Communion for granted, I sent you to a far-away Islamic country at war with your country.

'Lord, I am sorry for jumping to the end of that time, but after returning from Afghanistan for the last time in November 2013, I realized that you sent me there to experience a true culture of death, to experience true hunger and thirst for righteousness.

Working as a surgeon in Kabul, I saw many cases of advanced cancers beyond any chance for cure, tropical diseases most Western doctors only read about in books, such as malaria, tuberculosis, cholera, and various parasitic infestations, such as leishmaniasis, hydatid disease. We pulled Ascaris lumbracoides worms out of several patient's livers. We removed massive goiters and saw large facial masses encroaching upon and replacing what was once an eye. Other skin conditions we saw had destroyed parts of the face through a chronic ulcerative process. We saw bodies wasted from malnutrition and children with congenital deformities. And, we saw the devastating effects of poor obstetric care, women left with fistulas sitting for decades in their urine and feces, outcasts in their society.'

'My dear friend, you survived some close calls. Can you explain those?'

'Yes, Lord, I survived three incidents of carbon monoxide poisoning. Others did not survive such poisoning. Loose electrical wires in my basement apartment caused fires on two occasions. A Kam Air flight ran into a mountain on a snowy night, killing everyone aboard exactly one week after I had flown the same plane with the same airline crew, traveling in the same direction on another snowy night. On one occasion, driving through Kabul, gunfire opened on both sides of the road. Our driver gunned the engine and skillfully weaved through traffic out of harm's way. While leaving work one day, our team received a call about open gunfighting on my block, so we slept at the other team's house. Walking home one time at dusk, I was nearly attacked by seven stray dogs. On another night, a rocket mortar landed a block from my apartment. Suicide bombers damaged our hospital on three separate occasions. I received three direct death threats. I lost twelve friends, foreigners who served at our hospital in some capacity while I was there; all of them died violently, shot to death.'

'Lord,' I continued with tears, 'Your loving protection was all I had to rely on. However, while the risk to my physical being was not insignificant, the threat to my spiritual person was much more significant. You addressed this concern when you said.

"And do not be afraid of those who kill the body but cannot kill the soul; rather, be afraid of the one who can destroy both soul and body in Gehenna. (Matthew 10:28)"

'Yes, my dear friend, I said that and still do today.'

'Lord, on the occasions when I received you in Holy Communion at the Italian Embassy, I felt so thankful to be there, so thankful to have you under my roof. How could I not pray, *"Give us this day our daily bread."*

'My dear friend, keep praying for your daily bread as long as you live, and keep receiving me in the Eucharist as often as possible, for I say to you, *"Blessed are they who hunger and thirst for righteousness, for they shall be satisfied."*

Finding Jesus in Holy Matrimony While Unemployed

January 2014 – June 2014

Our home, Harrisburg, Pennsylvania

Imagine entering a small Catholic chapel sixteen years after your marriage in your wife's Protestant church, the Parkerford Church of the Brethren, in 1980. Her pastor officiated that first ceremony in front of several hundred family and friends. At this second ceremony in 1996, a priest officiates in front of one witnessing Catholic couple. After you exchange your vows, the priest prays, "Holy Father, who formed man in your own image, male and female, you created them, so that as husband and wife, united in body and heart, they might fulfill their calling in the world; O God, who, to reveal the great design you formed in your love, willed that the love of spouses for each other should foreshadow the covenant you graciously made with your people, so that, by fulfillment of the sacramental sign, the mystical marriage of Christ with his Church might become manifest in the union of husband and wife among your faithful; Graciously stretch out your right hand over these your servants Linda and Richard, we pray, and pour into their hearts the power of the Holy Spirit. Grant, O

Lord, that, as they enter upon this sacramental union, they may share with one another the gifts of your love and, by being for each other a sign of your presence, become one heart and one mind."

Jesus speaks, and you hear, *"Blessed are the merciful!"*

You and your wife pray, *"Forgive us our trespasses, as we forgive those who trespass against us."*

Jesus answers, 'My dear lovers, how generous you are. You have taken vows to have and to hold each other from this day forth for better, for worse, for richer, for poorer, in sickness and in health, to love and to cherish, till death do you part. You are joined in Holy Matrimony.

However, keeping those vows will be extremely difficult. Living together for so many years, you will encounter every internal rough spot, every facet of unpleasantness in each other. You will have a long life together to learn the difficult lessons of forgiving and receiving forgiveness. You must learn supernatural generosity, but do not worry; I am at the center of your sacramental marriage. As you grow together in faith, hope, and love, I will sustain you through it all, and together, *"You shall receive mercy!"*

I respond, 'Yes, Lord, unfortunately, it hasn't always been this way with me. Can I talk to you about that?'

'Dear friend, I know how often you have failed to love your wife, keep sacred the oath you swore, defend her integrity, and lie down your life for her, but have faith; you have more time to change all that.'

'Lord, I have realized how much mercy my wife showed me. Why didn't she leave me? Some of her friends advised this. As a Protestant, why did she agree to have our marriage blessed by the Catholic Church? These were not easy actions for her.'

'So, my dear friend, show mercy to her for the rest of your life whenever and wherever you can.'

'I should add, Lord, that she went back to work, though this had not been in her long-term plans. My unemployment stemmed from my bad decisions in 2002, and the hard consequences continued to emerge and affect her. I recall asking how to provide for my wife and son. My wife and I discussed the idea of me reapplying for my medical license. Still, after several attempts with legal counsel, we realized that the surgical practice door was permanently closed.'

'Recall my words, then. 'I closed it, my dear friend, but that does not mean I want you to remain idle, living off a monthly unemployment check. I have work for you to do. I will keep you purposely and gainfully employed. Start memorizing the Sermon on the Mount and avail yourself of Confession, Holy Communion, and Holy Matrimony as often as you desire. Daily Mass, frequent confession, and authentic communication with your wife are your first three orders of business. Trust and obey me, and watch how I bless your marriage."

'Despite my anxiety about income, Jesus, your words filled me with joy. Lord, your love is all we had to sustain us. You have been beside us and in us, and on any given day, we can see You in each other when we look with eyes of faith. Furthermore, Lord, although I had left a culture of death in Afghanistan, you brought death into my life nine times between April 2014 and May 2017.'

'Yes, my friend, let's talk about this. It will do you good to be reminded of their truths.'

'Lord, three of the deaths involved a sister, daughter, and wife of three friends who lived within a minute's walk of my house.

I accompanied the surviving sister, parents, and husband to oncology appointments and meetings in the intensive care unit to help them navigate end-of-life care decisions.

Three other unexpected deaths provided me with a rapid replay of significant parts of my life: that of a childhood friend who died of a sudden heart attack, a close friend of my wife and me who also died of a heart attack, and a coworker murdered at the front gate of our hospital in Afghanistan. None of these deaths left my wife or me unaffected. Together, we mourned the death of people close to us, consoled their family, and found a reason to console each other during those critical months of reuniting our marriage after the turbulent days in Afghanistan. Shall I tell you about the other three deaths?'

'Not now, my dear friend. There will be time for that. Keep looking at me with eyes of faith, especially when death stares right into your face. And you, my friend, with your wife, will show mercy and receive mercy to and from each other and those around you. You will travel a long, fruit-filled journey together with your children and their children. The road will be difficult but full of joy. You will overcome many obstacles together. You will stay with each other in sickness and health, good and bad times. You will learn why God joins women and men in Holy Matrimony.

'Which is why, Lord, I must repeat,' *"Forgive us our trespasses, as we forgive those who trespass against us."*

' And I, my dear friend, conclude this conversation by repeating,' *"Blessed are the merciful, for they shall be shown mercy!"*

An Exegesis – Parts One through Five of Nine

We are crossing over the midpoint of my nine-part experience with the Beatitudes, the Lord's Prayer, and the Catholic Church's sacraments, so I pause to consider them briefly from a literary and functional perspective.

Firstly, we pause to consider why we discuss a nine-part experience. The answer to this question is easy to understand. Rather than debating the number of Beatitudes in the Sermon on the Mount- is it seven or eight - we focus on a facet that no one disputes- that Jesus said *Blessed are*, nine times. Thus, we look for nine corresponding parts to the Lord's Prayer. Similarly, rather than immediately fixating on the fact that the Church has seven sacraments, we start by applying them to the Beatitudes/Lord's Prayer formula to get a sense of how they might lead us.

Next, we note how Jesus used numerous literary mechanisms to help the careful listener or reader understand how He linked the Beatitudes with the Lord's Prayer, especially when we place them side by side with the sacraments.

Notice the similarity in rhythmicity when saying, *"theirs is the kingdom of heaven,"* the second half of the first Beatitude, and *"Our Father in heaven."* When we add the sacrament of Baptism, we see a functionally unifying theme: a newly adopted child of God naturally cries out to their Father in heaven.

Linking the mourning sinner of the second Beatitude with joyfully hallowing God's name seems odd until we consider the comfort every penitent receives in the sacrament of Confession after reconciling with God.

The literary link between the third Beatitude, which ends with the word 'earth,' is, at the very least, hinted at in the Lord's Prayer, where 'earth' precedes 'heaven.' In this third one, we also find the idea of progression from carnal and worldly to spiritual and heavenly. Confirmation, focusing on Christian maturity, links the third Beatitude with the third part of the Lord's Prayer functionally. The mission of the Church militant centers on manifesting God's will and seeing His kingdom established on earth as it is in heaven.

Admittedly, these are soft and subtle 'links,' perhaps too simplistic sounding. Some may want further evidence, things more plainly manifest before their eyes and ears, to make hard 'links' between the first three 'thirds,' which is where the three 'fourths' and the three 'fifths' come into play. What am I talking about?

The Church calls the Eucharist the 'source and summit of Christian life.' [2] Everything centers around the Eucharist, so we should expect to find a clear, solid, plain, manifest link between the fourth Beatitude and the fourth part of the Lord's Prayer, as we have divided it. And so we do. It isn't difficult to see how the words, *"Blessed are they who hunger and thirst for righteousness, for they shall be satisfied,"* relate to *"Give us this day our daily bread."* Furthermore, hunger is a basic and universal human drive, as evident to the newborn as it is to the dying. All of us depend on this autonomic visceral drive for survival. The link between the Beatitude and the Prayer is clear from the words themself.

Thinking sacramentally, they who hunger and thirst spiritually naturally seek the bread and wine of the Eucharist.

In the fifth pairing of a Beatitude and part of the Lord's Prayer, we can see the link in two easy ways, first in the word's meaning and second in the similarity of the two sentences' cadence. Those who give mercy receive mercy. Those who forgive are forgiven. Meditating on these two sentences carefully, we can see how God makes His gracious actions, showing mercy and forgiveness, contingent on the preceding actions of the person. Thus, we see a unique verbal formula leading us to contemplate why and how the fifth Beatitude explicates the fifth part of the Lord's pair and vice versa. Thinking sacramentally, what better time and place can God provide his children to learn these challenging life-long lessons than through the sacrament of Holy Matrimony, which brings a man and a woman together in a 'till-death-do-us-part' covenant with Jesus at the center, keeping the two persons joined together as one until death do them part?

Stepping back to look from a literary structural viewpoint, when we align the fourth and fifth Beatitudes in this manner with the fourth and fifth parts of the Lord's Prayer, we facilitate a nine-part pairing of the two pillars of truth. Aligning the fourth and the fifth pairs in this manner keeps us from dividing up the Lord's Prayer in other ways because there must be three parts to the Prayer preceding the fourth and four parts following the fifth.

Is it important to fuss over such details in the grand scheme? I think so. Why? Let's return to the first Beatitude to make another observation- namely that the reward of those who are poor in spirit is the kingdom of heaven, presently, here and now. Jesus wasn't in the first century, nor can we in the twenty-first speak of this first Beatitude as applying only to some future date. The reward is written in the present tense. Elsewhere, Jesus said other things that make it seem like the distance between heaven and earth is not so great after all.

"Asked by the Pharisees when the kingdom of God would come, he said in reply, "The coming of the kingdom of God cannot be observed, and no one will announce, 'Look, here it is,' or, 'There it is.' For behold, the kingdom of God is among you." (Lk 17:20-21)

But, can you hear the scorners and mockers? "Oh really? How cute- you say the kingdom of heaven is here today? Where? Have you read the news, you imbecile? Have you considered the state of our world today? We have wars and pestilences, hunger and poverty. We live in fantasy worlds created by technology. Artificial intelligence is the new bastion of hope. In our self-asserted freedom, we choose to kill the unborn, ravage the marriage covenant, and try to redefine man and woman. Oops- I just gave it away. It wasn't the atheist or agnostic I was quoting. I am quoting Christians, including myself.

For us Christians, as always, there is the temptation to complain. Why, Lord, won't you just answer our prayers and straighten out this mess? Lord, with all due respect, it sure looks like there is a vast chasm between heaven and earth, a reality that lies painfully before us in our time. To many, nay to most Christians in the world today, having heaven on earth seems like an impossible task, a pipe dream.

How might Jesus respond? I imagine Him saying something like this- 'Yes, the way from earth to heaven is a great distance off, but have you considered the state of my Church, of fractured Christianity? Can the unbelieving, hurting, or searching world even find the Church today? Which one should they choose? If they can't find the Church, you can be sure they will not find the way to heaven. And if they cannot find the way to heaven, you can be sure they are going to Hell. What are you going to do about it?'

We could say much more about this imaginary conversation, but I think it will be better, for now, to return to the other imaginary conversation. Suffice it to say, we professing Christians must work together to build a recognizable and unified Church if we ever hope to manifest God's will be done on earth as it is in heaven. Christians must build the Church on solid and level, manifestly plain ground. And what better place to start reunifying our understanding of God's truths than in the very first sermon of our Savior in the New Testament? The world needs truth unflinchingly boldly and fully explained. We need to start again where Jesus started. We must keep the Beatitudes and the Lord's Prayer properly oriented with the sacraments if we ever hope to see God's will be done on earth as it is in heaven.

Finding Jesus in the Anointing of a Sick Contemplative Path Builder

January 2014 – June 2014

Our home, Harrisburg, Pennsylvania

Imagine, many years after the days you memorized the Sermon on the Mount, you lie in bed, your body weakened from disease, a shell of what it had been. You have come to your last day on earth. A priest is with you. He anoints your forehead and palms with oil and says, "Through this holy anointing may the Lord in his love and mercy help you with the grace of the Holy Spirit. May the Lord who frees you from sin save you and raise you up." Jesus is there also and speaks comforting words, *"Blessed are the clean of heart."*

You respond, *"And do you lead us into temptation!"*

Jesus says, 'I have seen your pain. I know suffering and death often lead to despair and anger. I know if there ever is a time when you need to persevere in your faith, now is that time. Therefore, I bring the sacrament of the Anointing of the Sick, have anointed your forehead, and prayed for your complete healing. Only look at me with faith, hope, and love, and know I am healing you entirely, especially your soul. For soon, my beloved child, *"You shall see God!"*

You respond, 'Lord, it hasn't always been this way with me. Can I talk to you about that?'

Jesus responds, 'I know how often you have failed to love me, but through the prayers of others and the steadfast love of your wife, you always found your way back.'

'Lord, can I tell you something else that I did during the months of unemployment in addition to rebuilding my marriage and memorizing the Sermon on the Mount?'

'My dear friend. I know what you did. You built a rock path. Yes, we prompted you to do that. We gave you, a general surgeon who performed the last operation of his career in Afghanistan, who found himself unemployed for the first time in his life, something to do with your hands that would calm your spirit and induce a contemplative mood. God, the Father, Son, and Holy Spirit, had worked a marvelous miracle in your soul, had repaired or, perhaps I should say, replaced your heart of stone with a new one, fresh and vibrant, beating with warm-blooded life. We accomplished great healing through your first five experiences to appreciate the Beatitudes, the Lord's Prayer, and the sacraments, although you were still, at that time, not consciously aware of it.

When you returned from Afghanistan with its culture of death and suddenly found yourself unemployed, confronting more deaths of friends and family around you, it was as if you had just awoken from a long operation under general anesthesia. Internally, you felt something stirring. You were gazing at the world around you with new eyes. Images appeared fuzzy until they were focused, and you squinted spiritually when the bright lights of truth shone all about you. We, the Father, Son, and Holy Spirit, were gazing intently into your eyes and were thrilled at the moment of recognition when you sat up and said, 'Lord, is that you,' I said, finishing Jesus' sentence.

'Yes, dear friend, after a loving embrace, I mean many loving embraces in daily Mass, we gave you rehab exercises to facilitate your postoperative recovery. Your wife inspired you to do many handyman chores around the house, and we inspired you to create a rock path on one side of your house, which also needed restoration. As you were creating the rock path, digging holes, and placing rocks in the dirt next to your house, you started to contemplate all that had happened to you since you lost your medical license eleven years prior.'

'Yes, Lord, that's when you inspired me to memorize and contemplate the Sermon on the Mount. Of course, I started with the Beatitudes.'

'My friend, you haven't stopped contemplating it since then-little wonder that you saw the links between what you had experienced in life and the Beatitudes. Tell me, now, about the other three times you and your wife found occasions to console each other at the death of a loved one.'

'Lord, the first was the death of my mother, she who had led me to Mass as a child and back again to daily Mass as an adult. She died a slow, wasting, cancerous death on March 8, 2016. The second was the death of Don Gleichman, our friend and financial planner, the same man who led me back to the Catholic faith as an adult through a men's bible study and by bringing you to me, Lord, in the Eucharist every Sunday during my ten-month incarceration. He died suddenly of a heart attack on May 5, 2017. Needless to say, he occupied a very special place in my heart, the spiritual brother coming alongside the spiritual mother to draw me closer to you.'

'And the ninth, the last, who according to earthly times was actually the first. Tell us about him, my dear friend.'

'I might not have thought about Richard Collin Manning during these days, but you ensured my wife and I did. How could we not think about him when my mother died exactly thirty-three years after the day he was born on March 8, 1983? And, how could we not think about him again when Don Gleichman died exactly thirty-four years after the day of his death on May 5, 1983?'

'My dear friend, never stop thinking of me, especially when death stares you in the face.'

'Lord, how can I ever stop thinking of you when you have given me words to ponder, words etched in stone on the gravestones of these three?'

'Yes, my dear friend, contemplate their words. 'Father, Not My Will, But Thine Be Done,' reads Don's. 'Patience Is A Virtue,' reads your mother's, and 'Let the Little Children Come to Me' reads your son's. Tend to today's problems, my dear friend, with your vision focused on me for your future with the innocent trust of a child grounded in a long past loving relationship.'

'Lord, the Beatitudes became my guiding light. Therefore, I immediately set out to memorialize what you had done, were doing, and will continue doing in my life. I didn't want to forget those precious days of awakening from anesthesia, so I built that rock path. It is my version of an altar, like Abraham, Isaac, and Jacob once built, to worship you. I created an image of your crown with three twisted, four to six-foot-long pieces of driftwood, which now lay strewn on either side of the path, your crown of thorns strewn on the earth after you conquered death and rose to accept your eternal heavenly crown.

I built a small raised flower bed from old railroad ties to symbolize the ancient Garden of Eden. Whenever it rains, water from the rooftops of the houses on either side of it flows down the path; its gurgling trickle is a reminder of the streams of life flowing from your throne. The wind chimes I hung remind the contemplative of the Holy Spirit, blowing where it will and when it will fresh life-giving air into our lungs and souls. I placed a statue of Mary standing at the front of the journey, and the curvy meandering path composed of rocks of different colors, sizes, and shapes is meant to lead those who walk it on a contemplative journey.'

'And lastly, my dear friend, you placed Richard Collin Manning's gravestone next to part of my crown. You and your wife finally had it made and placed it right where it needs to be today, to remember that he died, not even two months old, his body with its multiple congenital defects burning up with a fever of 107 degrees.'

'How could I miss what you were doing in my life, Lord, fixing my soul through the wounded suffering body of my son? How can I ever forget your works, fixing my wounded soul through your wounded, murdered, resurrected body?"

'My friend, his body is perfect now, and like mine, his is glorified. And we love your path. We love the many other paths you started to build at that time even more. The memory work you did and continue to this day serves another more physiologic purpose: rebuilding the neurological pathways of your brain through which you experience life. You memorized the first seven chapters of Matthew's gospel, including the lengthy forty-one-person genealogy leading to me. You memorized twenty-two proverbs, Psalm 19, and large chunks of Peter's and Paul's epistles.'

'Lord, I don't know about the biology of neurologic circuitry, but I can say this. Ever since I started the extensive memory work, the disruptive background noise in my mind, the negative thinking, harmful speculations, useless self-accusations, self-loathing, and self-pity no longer hold a place in my mind. You, Lord, have expelled Satan and his minions.'

'Amen, my dear friend. Now you understand why God gave you scripture. Keep memorizing it for the rest of your life, and we will keep filling your mind with profound mysteries, cleaning your heart, filling your soul with life that you might better see God.'

'Lord, I had a dream in those days in which I saw a hand pulling wires from one section of my brain and plugging them into another section. Was that the hand of God? Did I see the hand of God at work in my soul?'

'Indeed, my friend, we were and will continue rewiring your brain in the memory work. You had stopped the behavior that got you into trouble and had stopped frequenting the places that tempted you. Then we attacked the third and final source of your disordered appetites, the years of accumulated memories, feelings, and thoughts that could cause you to relapse. Still, as you point out correctly, we fixed your soul for the human person has a soul that cannot be reduced to mere physical elements and chemical processes.'

'Lord,' I said with tears, 'I am so happy you took over the operation, took the knife from this surgeon, and placed it in the hands of a master surgeon who anointed me with His healing balm. Oh, dear Lord, *"Lead me not into temptation."*

'Yes, my dear friend, and in this sickness and on your final day on earth, you will find peace when you receive one last anointing, one final earthly assurance, hear one last time, *"Blessed are the clean of heart, for they shall see God."*

Finding Jesus in Wounded Healers in the Office of Holy Orders

May 2014 through July 2019

Catholic Churches in Afghanistan, the Dominican Republic, Zambia, Kenya, Uzbekistan, Cuba, Malawi, India, United Arab Emirates, Nigeria, Ethiopia, and over twenty Catholic Churches in the United States

Imagine attending Mass, hearing priests from many nations speaking their native languages, and joyfully celebrating in the great wedding banquet they offer. They give the same greetings, read the same scripture, carry out the same liturgical actions, pray the same prayers, offer the same Lord, and bless with the same blessing in the name of the Father, Son, and Holy Spirit. They send you out into the world to carry on the same great commission. One day, you ask the Lord how can this be. How can many men of different nations, languages, and centuries celebrate the same Mass- the same wedding banquet? And then you see and hear Jesus. You watch Him extending His hands, those of a Bishop, over another man about to be ordained into the priesthood- he offers the prayer of consecration- bestows on him the office, Holy

Orders, to empower him to offer the Sacraments. While this is happening, Jesus says: *"Blessed are the peacemakers!"*

At the appointed time in the Mass, the priests and everyone else, those clergy presiding and laity participating pray, *"Deliver us from evil!"*

Jesus assures everyone in their hearts, saying, 'My dear friends, brothers, and sisters, my bride. I am with you always. You see me in the faces of loved ones and the faces of those who hate you, for whom you have become peacemakers. You, my bride, are more beautiful than the mind can conceive. See my helpers, priests, those who speak on my behalf, in my name. See them carrying out the duties of their office, Holy Orders, which the bishop gave them through the imposition of his hands when consecrating them for God's purposes in the Church, empowering them to bring you the sacraments, ensuring that you, *"Shall be called children of God!"*

You see Him in your mind's eye and with your real eyes with faith and rejoice at His ever-present mercy. You look into His eyes and see a familiar, smiling, loving face in every other face. You see Him in the face of your wife. She smiles back. On other days, you see Jesus' face in the face of those who have left the earth to meet Him and, in many others, yet journeying on earth to meet Him. In those moments, Jesus whispers, *"Blessed are the peacemakers!"*

You respond, 'Lord, it hasn't always been this way with me. Can I talk to you about that?'

Jesus responds, 'I know how often you have failed to love your neighbor, but through the work of many priests called to my service through the sacrament of Holy Orders, you continue returning to me in the confessional and receiving me in the Eucharist at Mass. You continue seeing me in your marriage, and once every year, you receive me through the sacramental of the blessing of throats celebrated on the feast day of Saint Blaise. In all this, you affirm your baptismal calling to be God's child and confirm yourself as a worthy soldier of Christ. You can always find your way back. I will be here always.'

'Lord,' in the five-year journey around the world from 2014 through 2019, you taught me much about your Church, its unity, catholicity, universality, history, and consistency. Still, most of all, you have shown me how present you make yourself to your bride, the Church, including me, as a member of your body, no matter where we go on earth.

'My dear friend, I also taught you a lot about yourself. I replaced your call to serve humanity as a surgeon with a call to serve humanity as a wounded healer. You have read Henri Nouwen's thoughts about making your wounds available as a source of healing for others. Has not your life been filled with wounds?'

'Yes, Lord, but primarily of my own doing, my mistakes, my sin.'

'Of course, my friend, sin damages your soul the most; It is the source of separation from God. Now you understand why I was stripped, beaten, crowned with thorns, nailed to a cross, and died. I did all of that to deliver the source of my sacramental life to the Church. When a Roman soldier pierced my stilled heart, blood and water spilled out, bringing forth the sacraments of the Eucharist and Baptism. As my mother looked on, she felt as Simeon had prophesized, a 'sword' piercing her heart. She and I were pierced *"so that the thoughts of many hearts may be revealed"* - our wounds, the source of healing for those who choose to receive my sacramental remedies.

In the same way, every ordained priest of my Church, those God has called to the office of Holy Orders, ministers sacramental life and healing through their wounds. The difference between them and me is that they are wounded because they have transgressed God's law, whereas I have never transgressed God's law. I was wounded and crucified to atone for their transgressions and those of all humanity.'

'Lord, what about those who sinned too many times to count?'

'My friend, I said already that we don't count the sins of a penitent sinner, but humans always will at some level in their conscience. They cannot forget as easily as we can. As the Psalmist wrote, *"For I know my transgressions; my sin is always before me."* (Psalms 51:5)

'Lord, what about me? I sincerely believe I am one of the greatest of sinners.'

'Your case is no different than the rest of humanity. Besides, to the extent that you understand the gravity of your past sins, so to that extent, you should work to pay God back, not for His good, but your own.'

'For my good, you say?'

'Yes, my friend, God does not benefit from your repentance. He likes it, nay; He loves it but does not need it. It adds nothing to His glory. You, however, can not so easily forget your sins, even after receiving God's forgiveness and His assurance that I have repaid what My Father's justice demands. In this case, you, a forgiven sinner, should do the penance prescribed by the priest.'

'Lord, I understand these ideas and usually leave the confessional joyful. Still, sometimes my conscience racks my sense of well-being.'

'My friend, that's Satan's work. When he brings the self-condemning thoughts into your mind for sins my Father has forgiven, use Satan's ploy against him. Let his accusations motivate you to serve God more ardently. Like every person who willingly receives my gift, let your sins and their painful consequences strongly undergird your communion with God. From that source of pain, continue to build everything the Father, Son, and Holy Spirit teach, building character one level at a time as you travel the path of the Beatitudes, supported by my beatific-centric Lord's Prayer and empowered by the sacraments, which do nothing more and nothing less than bring you into me and me into you. I repeat, *"Blessed are the peacemakers!"*

'Lord,' *"Deliver us from evil."*

My dear child, 'Have no fear, for you are among those about whom we say,' *"For they shall be called children of God."*

'God bless the clergy, Lord, set apart in Holy Orders. God bless all deacons, priests, bishops.'

'Yes, now you understand why my Father asked me to build the Catholic Church on earth. You have learned to pray for those who minister to the world in My name. God blesses the laity who run to my Church, to your true mother, that she may bestow abundant blessings on them through the sacraments. And, just as important, He blesses the Church's clergy through the prayers of the laity, so get busy praying.

Finding Jesus in the Sacramental Economy as a Child of the Beatitudes and the Lord's Prayer

May 2014 – Present

Wherever the Spirit Blows

Imagine yourself a sixty-year-old student in catechism class in your Catholic Church. The nun reads from the Catechism of the Catholic Church.

"The Church was made manifest to the world on the day of Pentecost by the outpouring of the Holy Spirit. The gift of the Spirit ushers in a new era in the 'dispensation of the mystery' the age of the Church, during which Christ manifests, makes present, and communicates his work of salvation through the liturgy of his Church, 'until he comes.' In this age of the Church, Christ now lives and acts in and with his Church, in a new way appropriate to this new age. He acts through the sacraments in what the common Tradition of the East and the West calls 'the sacramental economy; this is the communication (or 'dispensation') of the fruits of Christ's Paschal mystery in the celebration of the Church's 'sacramental' liturgy.'" (3)

After the nun completes the reading, Jesus says: *"Blessed are they who are persecuted for the sake of righteousness!"*

You and the universal Catholic Church militant look up in fear and bewilderment. You ask, 'Lord, how ought we to pray for this persecution?'

Jesus responds through the priest acting in the person of Christ as he prays.

"Deliver us, Lord, we pray, from every evil, graciously grant peace in our days, that, by the help of your mercy, we may be always free from sin and safe from all distress, as we await the blessed hope and the coming of our savior, Jesus Christ!"

You and the universal Catholic Church, militant, suffering, stand silently before the throne of God. Jesus continues speaking. *"for theirs is the kingdom of heaven."*

You respond, 'Lord, it has never been this way with me. Can I talk to you about that?'

Jesus responds, 'I know how you fear suffering and death.'

'Lord,' you say with a glimmer of hope, 'are you promising to protect my family and me from all bodily harm, pain, and suffering? If so, I'll take it because I am not seeking a martyr's death for them or myself. Still, how, then, can they and I suffer for the sake of righteousness?'

'My dear friend. Remember what I said about sin. Sin, more than anything, is that which harms you, what separates you from me. Remember what I said in Afghanistan about not fearing those who kill the body but cannot kill the soul; rather, be afraid of the one who can destroy both soul and body in Gehenna. Look closely at the prayer, *"that we may be always free from sin and safe from all distress."* You can only suffer for righteousness when you are free from mortal sin. There is no other way.'

'Lord, why did you not include the embolism within the Prayer you taught the disciples to pray when they asked how to pray? Why does it not appear in Matthew or Luke's gospel?'

'Having read the gospels, you know that at the start of my three-year ministry, my disciples were not ready to hear about my suffering, let alone that which awaited them. It wasn't until the time of the Last Supper I celebrated with them on the day before my arrest and subsequent crucifixion that it started to dawn on them that I was going to suffer.'

'Yes, Lord, but the gospels tell how all the apostles, except John, abandoned you in your hour of greatest need.'

'Yes, they did, but thankfully, they changed, or I should say, the Holy Spirit changed them at Pentecost. And then, they embraced the suffering that awaited them, as did others who followed. You know the Apostle Paul's part in this- how he went from a persecutor of my disciples, including Stephen, the first to follow me after my crucifixion, even as John the Baptist preceded me in his martyrdom. In both cases, these men suffered for the sake of righteousness.'

'And so too, Lord, history tells us did thousands of Christians after them in the first three centuries after your death choose death with righteousness instead of sin with spiritual death.'

'Yes, and so will you if My Father gives you the honor.'

'Gives me the honor, you say?'

'Yes, but as I see fear in your eyes at the mere mention of martyrdom, dear friend, let's return to the words of the Catechism of the Catholic Church.

"In this age of the Church, Christ now lives and acts in and with his Church, in a new way appropriate to this new age. He acts through the sacraments in what the common Tradition of the East and the West calls 'the sacramental economy;' this is the communication (or 'dispensation') of the fruits of Christ's Paschal mystery in the celebration of the Church's 'sacramental" liturgy.'"

'I see the words again, Lord, but don't see how they lead me to embrace martyrdom. Can you explain their meaning?'

'Of course- as the Church contemplated that ever-accumulating suffering, the meaning of the embolism became clear. The Church's ministers came to understand that when they celebrate the liturgy of the New Covenant in my name, replacing the flesh and blood of the Passover lamb with the bread, my body, and the wine, my blood, they were manifesting in the office of Holy Orders, its primary purpose, to celebrate my passion and resurrection in memory of me. The Church, in its liturgies and in its suffering, came to understand that I am with them, praying through them the words of the embolism.'

'Lord, how do those of us who don't aspire to suffer martyrdom as have so many Christian saints after them- how do we suffer for the sake of righteousness worthily?'

'My dear friend, have you not suffered disappointments, rejections, failures, and yes, pains in your body? I am not asking you to be crucified upside down, fed to lions willingly, or stand firm as your body ignites in flames. All I am asking you to do now is willingly suffer life's many daily hardships without complaining, plotting revenge, or becoming bitter.'

You silently contemplate how far you have come but how much further you need to go on this road to holiness. Jesus hears your prayer-filled thoughts even if you have only groaned them inaudibly and repeats through the priest,

"Deliver us, Lord, we pray, from every evil, graciously grant peace in our days, that, by the help of your mercy, we may be always free from sin and safe from all distress, as we await the blessed hope and the coming of our savior, Jesus Christ!"

You stand silent in front of Jesus, who repeats, *"Blessed are they who suffer for the sake of righteousness, for theirs is the kingdom of heaven."*

Finding Jesus by Suffering Joyfully Through, In, and With Him

May 2014 – Present

Wherever Jesus Leads

Imagine yourself attending daily Mass and obediently attending daily to your wife and family, friends, and enemies. You have read and reread innumerable times the ninth and last *'Blessed are'* sentence from the beginning of the Sermon on the Mount. For nearly a decade, you have memorized and visualized every word from that sermon daily. You close your eyes to visualize them again and hear a voice. Jesus says:

"*Blessed are you when they insult you and persecute you and utter every kind of evil against you [falsely] because of me. Rejoice and be glad, for your reward will be great in heaven. Thus they persecuted the prophets who were before you.*"

You and the universal Catholic Church, militant, suffering, and triumphant, raise your voices and shout out the doxology after the priest prayed the embolism.

"*For thine is the kingdom, the power and the glory, now and forever, amen!*"

You realize with a start that Jesus, with the last of His nine *'Blessed are'* utterances, has spoken directly to you and his entire body, the Church, making personal in the second person what He said eight other times impersonally in the third person to the whole world. He knows you, and you know Him. She, the Church, knows Him, and He knows her. You thought you knew Him at the humble start of the journey, and indeed you did, but you have come to know Him better after each phase of the journey. You have moved away from the false allures of flesh-limited relating, the phony fantasies of self-aggrandizement, and the imaginary foes to battle. You have moved to true intimacy, to knowing people and knowing God and to being known by people and to being known by God.

But, having traveled with Him and them, carrying His cross with Him and them, having relied on Him and them for a lifetime, you realize how little you know Him and them and how little you know yourself. Still, you know that He and they, His Church, will not leave you, never forsake you. His Church will prevail against all the evil offered by the world and Satan. You have heard and understood, *"And so I say to you, you are Peter, and upon this rock I will build my church, and the gates of the netherworld shall not prevail against it." (Mat. 16:18)*

As you consider these words, understanding that no other entity, institution, government, or nation has survived over the last two thousand years except Christ's Church, you stand firm on Christ's promise to Peter. You and the universal Catholic Church, militant, suffering, and triumphant, shout out boldly, defying Satan by giving God all the glory.

My dear reader, I don't know how to describe this scene, the one that unites heaven and earth, the prayers of the saints who departed earth and those remaining on earth, the Wedding Supper of the Lamb, the Mass in every place and every time, so I have taken words from John's last book, Jesus' *Revelation* to stir up your imagination.

"One of the elders said to me, 'Do not weep. The lion of the tribe of Judah, the root of David, has triumphed, enabling him to open the scroll with its seven seals.' Then I saw standing in the midst of the throne and the four living creatures and the elders a Lamb that seemed to have been slain. He had seven horns and seven eyes; these are the [seven] spirits of God sent out into the whole world. He came and received the scroll from the right hand of the one who sat on the throne. When he took it, the four living creatures and the twenty-four elders fell down before the Lamb. Each of the elders held a harp and gold bowls filled with incense, which are the prayers of the holy ones. They sang a new hymn:

"Worthy are you to receive the scroll and to break open its seals, for you were slain and with your blood you purchased for God those from every tribe and tongue, people and nation. You made them a kingdom and priests for our God, and they will reign on earth.'

I looked again and heard the voices of many angels who surrounded the throne and the living creatures and the elders. They were countless in number, and they cried out in a loud voice:

'Worthy is the Lamb that was slain to receive power and riches, wisdom and strength, honor and glory and blessing.'

Then I heard every creature in heaven and on earth and under the earth and in the sea, everything in the universe, cry out:

'To the one who sits on the throne and to the Lamb be blessing and honor, glory and might, forever and ever.'

The four living creatures answered, 'Amen," and the elders fell down and worshiped.' (Revelation 5:5-14)

Continuing the Exegesis – Parts Six and Seven

In the exegesis started earlier in this book, we left off stressing the importance of ecumenicalism. How appropriate, then, that we left off at the fifth Beatitude, the fifth part of the Lord's Prayer and the sacrament of Holy Matrimony. In the past five hundred years, Protestants and Catholics have said and done many things to each other that are anything but merciful. Instead of faith, hope, and love, they have given each other many reasons to ask each other for forgiveness. So, let's pick up where we left off, at the Sixes.

There are three sixes we need to look at. First, *"Blessed are the clean of heart, for they shall see God."* Second, *"And lead us not into temptation."* Third, the sacrament of the Anointing of the Sick. It isn't hard to understand Jesus' use of the metaphor of a clean heart. When we sin, we make our hearts dirty. In the same way, it is not hard to understand why we sinners must pray *"lead us not into temptation,"* for we know how prone we are to sin. Indeed, the humility of the first Beatitude and the mourning of the second have helped us develop an acute sensitivity to our proclivity to sin.

The sixth sacrament addresses our sinful predisposition at times in life when we need it most. Yes, that can mean when death and suffering confront us personally or when they descend on someone close to us. Imagine the young couple who learn that their six-month-old has a terminal disease - this just happened in our sphere of friends. One day, they are living a clean, hope-filled married life, and the next day, it seems their entire world is crashing down. It isn't hard to imagine anger, questioning, and doubt towards God in this scenario.

How this couple or any of us react to life's apparent injustices is a deeply personal matter between God and each individual. Will our anger and doubts lead to resentment and bitterness, or will they drive us to depend on Him all the more? It is, indeed, a matter of critical importance, for as Jesus said, *"Be sober and vigilant. Your opponent the devil is prowling around like a roaring lion looking for [someone] to devour." (1 Peter 5:8)*

The sixth sacrament in our scheme links physical suffering with spiritual suffering, bringing it straight to the 'heart' of the matter, as Jesus said. It refocuses our spiritual vision to continue looking for and seeing God, especially when most needed.

The seventh Beatitude, *"Blessed are the peacemakers, for they will be called children of God,"* builds on this last point of the three Sixes. There have always been two large groups of people in the world since the original sin: those who walk without and away from God and those who walk toward and with God. Those who will to be called God's children fix their eyes on God, clean their hearts by pleading to avoid sin's temptations, and humbly receive His anointing when spiritually sick. These grateful ones promote peace. It makes perfect sense that they pray to be delivered from evil, from the evil one.

On the other side, we have a group of people who do not will to be called children of God. Whether or not they realize it, when they reject God, they are choosing Satan. Their sullied hearts cloud their vision. They don't see a remedy or want one, at least most of the time, unless God's grace breaks through and they choose to start walking with and toward Him. That option is always open, even for the most hardened and seemingly evil among us, which is why we are called to love and pray for them and any other enemies, as Jesus reminds us a bit later in His Sermon.

Here's the truth. All of us have been there at one time or another, angry at, rejecting, and even cursing God. The Church tells us that from the moment of our birth, in our fallen state, we cannot return to God on our own power. The Apostle Paul, once known as Saul, who violently persecuted Christians, couldn't have said it more clearly. *"All have sinned and are deprived of the glory of God." (Romans 3:23)* Nor could he have given the solution with more clarity. *"They are justified freely by his grace through the redemption in Christ Jesus." (Romans 3:24)* God often works through those who reject Him, even as we have seen here, through His most notorious enemies.

Furthermore, and more focused on Holy Orders, God has always worked through sons He has chosen and set apart to bring His gifts to the world so the world can bring gifts back to Him. Abel brought an acceptable gift back to God. Cain did not. Noah built an altar, sacrificed clean birds and animals, and offered burnt offerings to God. The aroma pleased God, who then blessed Noah with the rainbow covenant. King Melchizedek, likely Noah's firstborn son, Shem, was the first named priest and foreshadowed Christ's priesthood by rewarding Abraham with bread and wine after he righteously rescued his nephew, Lot. Abraham responded by giving him *"a tenth of everything."* God made a covenant with Abraham to multiply his descendants as numerous as the stars, give them land, and make his descendants a blessing to all nations.

Abraham, Isaac, and Jacob built altars and offered sacrifices to thank God and to commemorate His saving works and covenant. After delivering Israel from Egyptian bondage through signs and miracles, including the Passover, God instructed Moses to create a priesthood to minister gifts and sacrifices between God and Israel to celebrate this miraculous deliverance forever. King David acted like a priest, bringing forth a gift, the sacrifice of praise, when he wore a linen ephod and danced before the ark of God as it was brought to the temple in Jerusalem.

God the Father chose God the Son. *"For to which of the angels did God ever say, : You are my son; this day I have begotten you"? Or again, "But to which of the angels has he ever said: "Sit at my right hand until I make your enemies your footstool"? Are they not all ministering spirits sent to serve, for the sake of those who are to inherit salvation?" (Heb. 1:5 and 1:13-14)*

Jesus chose to obey God's call on His life. *"He advanced a little and fell prostrate in prayer, saying, "My Father, if it is possible, let this cup pass from me; yet, not as I will, but as you will." (Mat. 26:39)*

Jesus grew up worshipping in the Jewish synagogue and participating completely in first-century Judaism's celebrations, liturgies, and ordinances. He transformed the mode but never rejected the idea of priestly service. Rather, He affirmed and elevated the purpose of priests, namely that of receiving and giving gifts from God to His people and back again. He instituted the sacrament of Holy Orders. (See Acts 1:8, Jn. 20:22-23, 1 Tim. 4:14 and 2 Tim. 1:6-7)

In His New Covenant Church, God works through men who choose Him after firm deliberation and prayerful discernment, answering His call to serve Him as a minister to His people. A thorough consideration of Mat. 16:18- 19 and Mat. 18:18, wherein Jesus gave Peter the keys to the kingdom of heaven, assuredly deserves a deeper and more thorough consideration than I can offer; likewise, concerning Jesus' words in John 20:19-23, wherein we find Jesus again bestowing on the apostles the authority to forgive sins.

I want to make just one observation that I find interesting and telling concerning the peacemaking sons of the seventh Beatitude. It concerns John's account of Jesus' use of the phrase, *"Peace be with you,"* which He said the first time in John 20:19. Significantly, when Jesus says, *"Peace be with you,"* a second time, He follows with, *"As the Father has sent me, so I send you."*

Clearly, the mandate to minister in God's Church includes being a peacemaker. God's chosen ministers in the Church bring peace to the world really and truly, not by merely wishing for it or speaking out for peace on earth at rallies, as good as that is, but by actualizing it whenever they administer a sacrament. In Baptism, Confession, Confirmation, Holy Communion, Holy Matrimony, and the Anointing of the Sick, the Church rebirths, reconciles, re-energizes, refuels, reunites, and resurrects sinners when that time comes. She draws sinful humans away from Satan, the Father of lies, hatred, and death, and towards God, the Father of love and life, even if it means suffering for and dying for the sake of righteousness. In Holy Orders, the seventh sacrament, the Church receives through, with, and in the name of God the Father, Son, and Holy Spirit, her called sons equipped to bring Jesus sacramentally to the world one century after the next.

Pausing to Reflect on Sevens Before Considering Eights and Nines

Before moving on to complete the eighth and ninth parts of the exegesis, I want to anticipate some lingering questions about adding anything to seven. Seven is the number of perfection. God created the world in seven days. God instructed Moses, *"For six years you may sow your field, and for six years prune your vineyard, gathering in their produce. But during the seventh year the land shall have a sabbath of complete rest, a sabbath for the LORD, when you may neither sow your field nor prune your vineyard. You shall count seven weeks of years—seven times seven years—such that the seven weeks of years amount to forty-nine years"* (Lev 25:3,4,8)

God commanded Joshua to lead Israel into the promised land and begin its Canaan conquest by marching around Jericho for seven days- *"with seven priests carrying ram's horns ahead of the ark. On the seventh day march around the city seven times, and have the priests blow the horns. When they give a long blast on the ram's horns and you hear the sound of the horn, all the people shall shout aloud. The wall of the city will collapse, and the people shall attack straight ahead."(Jos. 6:4-5)*

Peter asked, *"Lord, if my brother sins against me, how often must I forgive him? As many as seven times?"* Jesus responded, *"I say to you, not seven times but seventy-seven times." (Mat. 18:21-22)*

The Bible contains many other sevens associated with God's dealings with His people. Indeed, the Church has seven sacraments. Why continue adding two more parts to the Lord's Prayer and conceptualizing the sacraments in nine parts? I'll offer a few ideas, but you should know that my answer is incomplete.

We noted in an earlier chapter that **Jesus** said, *"Blessed are"* nine times. But let me say it again slightly differently. **God** said *Blessed are* nine times. Let me continue. **God** said, *"Blessed are"* nine times as He embarked on a three-year earthly ministry to make a new covenant in His name.

How did Jesus' disciples understand his words at the Last Passover Supper of the old covenant? - *"This cup is the new covenant in my blood, which will be shed for you." (Lk. 22:20)* What did *"new covenant"* mean to His disciples, descendants of the nation through which the first creation account and the first covenant came? We don't have to look far, for we can find the answer in the gospels and epistles they wrote. See how the Apostle John revealed his understanding of Jesus' *"new covenant"* as a new creation. *"In the beginning was the Word, and the Word was with God, and the Word was God. He was in the beginning with God; all things were made through him, and without him was not anything made that was made." (John 1:1-3)*. John's intention is clear. We should think of Jesus' mission, the *"new covenant"* in His blood, as nothing less than a new creation. Consider words from the Apostle Paul also conveying the same truth, now applied to individual Christians.

"So whoever is in Christ is a new creation: the old things have passed away; behold, new things have come." (1 Cor. 5:17)

With these references to a new creation in mind, I want to look briefly at the old creation described in the first Genesis creation narrative. When we look there with the idea of counting, an idea modeled throughout the narrative, we find something quite interesting. While God created the universe in seven days and humanity on the sixth day, He created man with His eighth creative utterance, by which I mean He spoke. Genesis spells it out clearly by repeating the phrase, *"Then God said,"* followed by whatever God created.

This three-word phrase, *"then God said,"* precedes the phrases: *Let there be light, and there was light, (Gen 1:3), and "Let there be a dome in the middle of the waters, to separate one body of water from the other." (Gen 1:6)* It also precedes the next five creative utterances in Genesis 1:9, 1:11, 1:14, 1:20, 1:24 until the author of Genesis uses the phrase for the eighth and final time when it precedes, *"Let us make human beings in our image, after our likeness. (Genesis 1:26)* Therefore, while God created man on the sixth day and blessed him on the seventh, He created man with His eighth creative utterance.

The other unique feature of the eighth creative utterance is that Genesis portrays God referring to Himself as *Us,* which the Church has long understood as the first scriptural reference to the Trinity. Indeed, God's eighth creative utterance is special because He made humanity in His image with the capacity to understand personhood. We aren't mere creatures. We are people with souls who can see God in many ways, especially in the faces of other humans who are made in God's image. Thus, we see God appraising humanity alone as *"very good,"* whereas we see Him appraising the rest of creation throughout the Genesis narrative as merely *"good."*

Did Jesus show this high regard for humanity in His nine-part *"new creation"* utterances? I think the Genesis narrative supports this idea also. Consider God blessed the animals once, *"saying: Be fertile, multiply, and fill the water of the seas; and let the birds multiply on the earth."* God blessed humans one time also. *" God blessed them, and God said to them: Be fertile and multiply; fill the earth and subdue it. Have dominion over the fish of the sea, the birds of the air, and all the living things that crawl on the earth. (Gen. 1:28)* God offered one more blessing over everything at the first creation. *"God blessed the seventh day and made it holy because on it he rested from all the work he had done in creation." (Gen. 2:3)*

But see what Jesus did with the Beatitudes. He blessed nine times. He blesses at every stage of the process. And I believe He did that because He wasn't just creating humanity, of and on the earth. He is creating humanity in and for heaven. At least, that's how I see it, and I'm not alone. See the Apostle Paul's words again.

"But as it is written: What eye has not seen, and ear has not heard, and what has not entered the human heart, what God has prepared for those who love him," this God has revealed to us through the Spirit." (1 Cor 2:9)

Returning to Mass to Complete the Exegesis – Parts Eight and Nine

After completing our exegesis of parts six and seven of the tripartite literary and functional construct, we paused to address possible objections to moving beyond seven's perfection by looking for eights and nines. We now return to the place where we had stopped. Perhaps it was not accidental. Perhaps we needed to stall before exegeting eights and nines to better collect ourselves before moving forward.

We had mentioned the idea of suffering, even to death, for the sake of righteousness. We have arrived at the eighth Beatitude in our exegesis, which, for obvious reasons, none of us was looking forward to. Suffering is not on my bucket list. What's worse, from the standpoint of the tripartite construct we have been following, we have run out of parts to the Lord's Prayer, as we find it in Matthew's gospel and sacraments, as we find them in the Catholic Church. 'Lord,' we might ask, 'would you deprive us now of a prayer to say, of a sacrament to live in, now, at this juncture, as we consider suffering?'

With perhaps growing desperation, we look around. Concerning the prayer, it is eminently clear that we cannot return to somehow squeeze more out of the earliest parts of the Lord's

Prayer. For instance, why not divide the third part into two, one for seeing God's will be done on earth and one part for seeing His kingdom come in heaven? No, the twin pillars following the third have fixed the parts of the prayer where we have found them, three before the fourth and four after the fifth.

How about the remainder of the Lord's Prayer- *"And do not subject us to the final test, but deliver us from the evil one"* - Can we squeeze more parts out of that? Unfortunately, we can't do that without violating the Prayer's sentence structure, tearing apart verbs from nouns and nouns from prepositions. Concerning the sacraments, the Catholic Church long ago declared there are seven and reaffirmed the same in numerous councils and decrees. That count will never change. Has anyone else tried to link the Beatitudes and the Lord's Prayer? Fortunately for us, the answer to that question is yes.

History reveals that many ancient and modern scholars have wrestled with pairing the Beatitudes and the Lord's Prayer. Two of the Church's greatest Saints, Augustine of Hippo and Thomas Aquinas, taught some ideas that can help us think about this apparent problem of having only seven parts in the Lord's Prayer and seven sacraments when we need nine. In his *Thomas Aquinas On The Beatitudes - Reading Matthew, Disputing Grace and Virtue, Preaching Happiness*, Anton Ten Klooster discusses Thomistic thinking as it relates to the question of seven, eight, or nine Beatitudes. Quoting Thomas and sharing his own thinking, Klooster writes, "The eighth beatitude would be "Blessed are they who are persecuted for the sake of justice, for theirs is the kingdom of heaven" (Mt. 5:10). Aquinas again follows Augustine when he states that this is not a subsequent step toward happiness, but that it "indicates the perfection of all preceding beatitudes." The believer who endures persecution shows that he possesses the fullness of the beatitudes... When considering the beatitudes as a series of nine, the final beatitude would be: 'Blessed are you when they insult you and persecute you and utter every kind of evil against you (falsely) because of me.' (Mat 5:11)" [4]

What seems apparent from the second half of both the first and eighth Beatitudes and is consistent with Klooster's analysis of Aquinas' words is that they serve as literary bookends, so to speak. When one finishes reading the eighth Beatitude, they understand their overall goal: possessing the kingdom of heaven. See how Jesus spoke it in the present tense, "Theirs **IS** the kingdom of heaven." Using the same phrase, Jesus shows that we already possess heaven, the reward of the first Beatitude, when manifesting poverty of spirit, humility, and the call of the first Beatitude. Thus, whether by remaining poor in spirit or by suffering willingly for righteousness, we manifest the kingdom of heaven.

In contrast, Jesus spoke the reward of the second through seventh Beatitudes in the future tense. "They who mourn **will be comforted**, *the meek* **will inherit**, *the spiritually hungry* **will be satisfied**, *the merciful* **will be shown** *mercy, the clean of heart* **will see** *God and the peacemakers* **will be called.** Thus, the first half of all the Beatitudes exhort us to walk presently in their precepts while only the first, eighth, and ninth, as we shall see, promise the reward in the present. The second through the seventh promise their rewards in the future. In this present to future back to the present tense flow of nine sentences, we can discern a spiritual life-guiding, life-long step-by-step instruction manual within the Beatitudes. We have everything needed to bring heaven to earth in the nine Beatitudes here and now while straining to find heaven on earth in the future. Thus, in the fourth century, Gregory of Nyssa called the Beatitudes "Jacob's ladder." [5]

It is easy to miss a very important mandate of the Beatitudes if we fail to recognize how the eighth recapitulates the first seven. One cannot manifest any of the first seven Beatitudes if one rejects any one of them. The literary structure of the Beatitudes does not allow it. The eighth summarizes the first seven, not just the first or any other individual Beatitude. It summarizes them all as one unit of teaching. We haven't fully received or appreciated God's comfort when mourning if we never intend to show mercy to others.

Similarly, one does not fully receive or appreciate any of the first seven sacraments if one rejects any one of them. Thus, when thinking of how to enumerate the sacraments, we can find an analogy in the Church's teachings- She dispenses seven sacraments but summarizes them with the phrase "sacramental economy." Read Article 1076 of the Catechism of the Catholic Church again on pages 105 and 106 of this book. In the same way that the eighth Beatitude summarizes the first seven Beatitudes, the phrase "sacramental economy" summarizes the seven sacraments. The Church forbids Catholics to receive Holy Communion if they have sinned mortally and refuse to avail themselves of the sacrament of Penance. The same applies to Catholics who marry outside the sacrament of Holy Matrimony, who should not receive the Eucharist. We can't pick and choose which of the Church's teachings we will adhere to.

Okay, so we have a way to pair eight Beatitudes with the Church's sacraments. We will get to the ninth shortly, but now we must ask about the seeming shortage of parts in the Lord's Prayer. Ironically, the idea to include the embolism and doxology came to me partly from my twelve years of worshipping in a Protestant denomination that recites the Lord's Prayer every Sunday and automatically includes the doxology, as most do. When I returned to the Catholic Church, I again continued praying the Lord's Prayer weekly, but with one very noticeable difference. We don't say the doxology right after praying *'deliver us from evil,'* when Jesus stopped the prayer as found in the Sermon on the Mount. We only pray the doxology after the priest prays the embolism.

It was only a matter of time after I had returned to Mass and memorized the Sermon on the Mount until I saw how the embolism and doxology complete the Lord's Prayer in a way that allows the Church to complete her response to Jesus' nine Beatitudes. Thus, we have identified parts eight and nine of the Lord's Prayer and found an 'eighth sacrament.'

What about the ninth sacrament? I like to think of it this way. Music, for some mystical reason, works through a system of notes based on an octave, eight notes in various scales, working in concert to provide the musician with a template to follow when singing or playing an instrument. The written notes on the musical page provide complete instructions, yet they can never make music unless a human being comes along and uses them for their God-given purpose. Likewise, the eight Beatitudes are the working system of octaves to be repeated throughout our lives, instructing us, God's children, how to live lives that glorify Him, how to praise Him in music, and every facet of our lives.

Unless the Beatitudes find a place in our lives, they mean nothing, for they do not make music apart from finding expression through beings with eternal souls. Let me state the idea positively in terms of the Trinity. With the Holy Spirit, Jesus Christ seeks to establish the Beatitudes in our minds, entrench the Lord's Prayer in our hearts, and ensconce Himself in our souls, hidden in the sacraments and us, so that we, the Church, with God the Son and God the Holy Spirit, may manifest praise and glory to God the Father.

Our exegetical commentary started by bringing two pillars of Christian truth, the Beatitudes and the Lord's Prayer, into proximity with each other. Well, Jesus did that in the Sermon on the Mount. Then, rather than debating the number of Beatitudes Jesus spoke, we focused on an aspect of the Sermon on the Mount that no one disputes. He started the first nine sentences with the words, *Blessed are.*

Using nine as a common denominator, we found nine numerators and a way to conceptualize the Lord's prayer and the sacraments in nine parts. For mathematicians seeking numerical formulas to express truth, let me offer three. Note that Bs stands for Beatitudes, LPs for the Lord's Prayer, and Ss for sacraments. $9 \text{ Bs} / 9 \text{ LPs} = 1$. $9 \text{ Bs} / 9 \text{ Ss} = 1$. $9 \text{ LPs} / 9 \text{ Ss} = 1$. $1 + 1 + 1 = 3$ and three is a Trinity. Sorry if that seems corny. I have gotten into this habit of using numbers and letters to create easy ways to remember concepts. I guess it's part of what makes me human.

More to the point, in the tripartite literary functional construct, we brought the Beatitudes, the Lord's Prayer, and the sacraments into the place where they started and where they find their fullest expression, namely, in the Mass. Scripture alludes to these three critical parts of worship in the Church's early life, as found in the *Acts of the Apostles.*

"They devoted themselves to the teaching of the apostles and to the communal life, to the breaking of the bread and to the prayers." (Acts 2:42)

In her earliest days, the Church in her worship assemblies read scripture, listened to the preaching of Christ's disciples, prayed, and broke bread together. The Beatitudes, much more scripture, the Lord's Prayer, and many other prayers became part of the Church's worship and liturgies, including the Mass we celebrate today. While the Catholic Mass has evolved over the centuries, it has always contained these three essential parts: scripture reading, prayer, and breaking the bread.

The Mass I have participated in for nearly my entire life is based on Pope Paul VI's liturgical reforms from the 1960s or some derivative thereof. It was then that the embolism and doxology were definitively inserted into the liturgy.

Thus, it was the Mass, that ancient celebration, that the Church discerned from the essence of Jesus' teachings, including His example at the Last Supper, in which the Sacrament of the Eucharist was first brought into close proximity with the Beatitudes and the Lord's Prayer. In other words, I did not make this stuff up. I have merely shared what my eyes have seen, my hands have touched, my tongue has tasted, and, oh yeah, what my ears have heard in Mass all my life, especially nearly every day for the past ten years when I was repeating the Sermon on the Mount daily.

Returning to the Church Parking Lot

August 7, 2023, at approximately 7:40 am

Holy Name of Jesus Church Parking lot

We return, at last, to my woes on the morning following the wondrous three-day men's retreat hosted by Corpus Christi Church at Saint Mary's College and Seminary and the occasion on which I spit out and lose Jesus immediately after receiving Him at Mass. Having turned left out of the hardware store parking lot, I made two more lefts and then a right turn to park my car near the small chapel. The joy of the weekend was not on my mind. I felt carelessly negligent and deeply saddened. How could I be so cavalier with the Word of God? Was God teaching me something about the sacramental Word made flesh or about His written word made scripture- how carefully one must handle them? I decided against seeing Father Quinlan for the moment. Instead, I returned to the place outside the small chapel, retracing as best I could my steps from the chapel door, across a small patch of grass, and onto the asphalt pavement.

A juncture of wet and dry pavement allowed me to find the general area of concern quickly. I squatted on my haunches to resume the search. I was encouraged when I found a tiny fragment of a plant I had seen before, confirming my intuition about being close to the area of concern. I stared at the stony variegated mosaic for another five minutes until my eyes glazed and started to water. I explored its surface with my fingertips, focusing my mental capacities to perceive with my mind's eye what the tips of my fingers were conveying about the surface on which they rested. I looked around at the five-by-seven-foot patch and considered that we hadn't found the host fragment earlier. My heart sank. How sad! I had spit out that which is more precious than anything else on Earth or in the rest of the universe, for that matter.

Reeling from the juxtaposed weekend high and the Monday morning low, I then thought of the man who had marveled at the return of his youthful vision after cataract surgery. 'I missed it, Lord. You had him tell me that story so I could ask him for assistance at just the right time. You provided the answer, and I didn't listen.'

Then, I thought of my three-year-old grandson and his ability to find small shark teeth on the beach. My wife and I had spent a week at the seashore with him and his family in mid-July. We all marveled at his shark-tooth-finding ability and concluded he had two advantages: his eyes were younger and closer to the hidden objects. I adjusted my glasses, lowered my head, and intently peered at the ground for another five minutes. Nothing new appeared visually- more variegated yellow/white stones. Nothing new appeared tactilely- more hard stones.

Recalling again the Mass readings that morning and wallowing in the seemingly futile effort to find Jesus, I prayed a final prayer as I should have prayed initially. I closed my eyes and asked Saint Anthony of Padua for help. 'Saint Anthony, please come to my assistance. Surely, you will help me find our Lord.' I felt dizzy as

I prayed, still squatting on my haunches with closed eyes. Perhaps the blood had drained out of my head. Perhaps the heaviness of the morning had beaten me down. Feeling like I would lose my balance and fall, I quickly stretched out my left hand to the ground, slightly behind me, to steady myself, eyes still closed. I must have felt something as my index finger touched the asphalt, but I can't say so definitively. In any case, for some reason, I lifted my hand, opened my eyes, and examined my index finger, and then, I saw it: a small, 3- to 4-millimeter-sized round ball of a wet, saliva-soaked bit of white mushy stuff. My first reaction was disbelief. Could this be that small bit of the Eucharist? A moment of doubt- but wait, had it been on my finger the entire time, and I was just now noticing it?

No, I had seen it fall out of my mouth in front of me. Besides that, how could it have stayed on my finger? My left hand had reached into my pocket to get the keys to my jeep, opened the door to get in, held the steering wheel, opened the door to get out, lifted the rear hatch of the jeep, grabbed, and carried a propane tank, opened and closed the jeep door again, put the keys in my pocket and then resumed the search. This had to be the same bit of Eucharist I had spit out. New feelings surfaced: relief, jubilation, awe, and then doubt again.

I gently touched and examined it with my right index finger, confirming its soft, sticky nature. When I slowly lifted my examining finger off the Eucharist, a small fraction, perhaps a third of the whole, broke away from the discovered whole but remained attached by a tiny thread of . . . saturated bread – hesitation - or . . . a wisp of the Eucharist saturated with my saliva – apprehension - or . . . the Lord's body – beyond comprehension! That's right- the kiss I refer to is more than symbolic, though it is that, too. It is more than spiritual in the sense of being without material substance, though it is that, too. The kiss I refer to is real, spiritual, sacramental, an unexplainable mystery. Haven't you ever wondered why Jesus put His fingers in the deaf and mute man's ears and then spit, presumably on His finger, before touching his tongue? Have you wondered why Jesus, in that same miracle, *"looked up to heaven and groaned, and said to him, "Ephphatha!" (that is, "Be opened!") (Mark 7:34)* Do you feel his passion, His suffering for that man at that moment?

Can you understand or at least imagine why I immediately stopped fractioning the host and rested it next to the larger piece on my left index finger sorrowfully, wondering if I had put my finger in Christ's wounds, feeling like doubting Thomas, needing still more evidence to bolster my faith?

And then, as with a kind of divine literary finality, I saw a minute black speck of asphalt between the two fragments, like a period at the end of a sentence, confirming where it had laid for forty minutes. The answer was final, but there was one more mandatory test, one more way to confirm who I had found undeniably. Without another thought, I put my left index finger in my mouth and received that solid, soft, undeniable confirmation. I know that taste. Yes, the small fragment had the same familiar taste as that which I had tasted nearly every day for the past ten years. I sucked on my right index finger in case any hidden fragments remained there and then did the same again with my left finger to ensure I ingested every particle. I expressed my sorrow to Jesus and my profound gratitude to Saint Anthony. I thanked the Lord for allowing me to finish consuming my daily bread for the day, exclamation point, and all.

After the Event

I realize the story of the lost and found Eucharist sounds farfetched to some of my readers, perhaps many non-Catholic ones. Honestly, the further I am removed from the event, the more incredible and almost unbelievable it seems to me. Within minutes after it happened, I asked myself if it really had happened. Then, I replayed the entire scene again from start to finish, in my mind, assuring myself of its authenticity. Perhaps because of my lingering doubt, I decided to tell someone immediately before I could chicken out and never tell anyone. As I drove by a coffee house on the way home, I saw a group of five men, two of whom had been in the gathering outside the chapel after Mass. I stopped and told them. When I got home, I told my wife. The following day, I told Father Quinlan after Mass. Over the next week, I told everyone else who had been at the gathering, including the three who had helped search for it. I told the other parish priest, Father Tritle as well. Everyone who had witnessed or participated in the search recalled the four of us stooping over a patch of concrete and were happy to have me answer their questions about what we were doing that morning and its happy outcome. Nearly everyone marveled. Nearly no one expressed doubt. A few expressed the belief that finding the bit of the Eucharist was a miracle.

I am not surprised that some have doubted the experiences' authenticity. Forget the table manners about not talking with your mouth full. How about another rule of your mother: never eat food off the floor, especially if it is wet, and didn't pass the five-second rule? I can hear the germophobes. 'You ate it after it lay on the ground for forty minutes- gross and stupid, by the way!' Well, yes, it may seem gross and stupid. However, the other option was to leave the Lord to get run over by a car or to be eaten by some wandering ants. What would you have done if it was in your power to resume the search? How long would I have searched? I don't know. I didn't have to pass this test beyond forty minutes.

More importantly, how would I do on a test about the readings from the Mass that morning? Not just a few times, but on many occasions, I have found confirmation of something God was trying to teach me in the Mass's readings on that particular day. Many Christians, Catholics, and Protestants have experienced the same.

The Mass's readings of that day had burned in my heart, loving but painful, as I left the asphalt parking lot for the first time that morning. They burned in my heart a second time that same morning, loving but consoling, as I drove out of the parking lot. It was my turn to walk with Jesus on the road to Emmaus, have scripture's burning truth confirmed by Jesus' sacramental presence, and see Him in the breaking of the bread. (See Luke 23)

I hope you will contemplate the August 7th, 2023, Mass readings on your own to discern how they might apply to the stories I have shared in this book, especially the lost and found story, and, more importantly, how they may apply to your life.

Searching for Jesus

One doesn't easily leave such experiences with the Word of God. Indeed, one doesn't leave them unaffected. The word of God, inscripturated and sacramental, always has an effect, either softening a heart to love Him more ardently or hardening it to resist Him more stubbornly. In this light, I felt compelled to share more about the early days after this one, asking what lessons we should take away from the morning of August 7, 2023. How should we search for Jesus?

My first lesson came from a fellow Knights of Columbus brother, the Grand Knight, sitting with the group I told at the coffee house – 'chew five times and swallow your food promptly, as your mother taught you.' There is a second lesson from our mothers, not surprisingly. Don't talk with your mouth full at the dinner table. In short, when approaching the Lord's table and receiving the meal Mother Church places before us, we must be fully prepared to receive Him. So far, so good.

Here are three more lessons. Saint Anthony is the Patron Saint of lost items. Catholics cannot argue with this. He loves Jesus. I hope no one will argue about this. Saint Anthony is alive and well, and he helped me find the Eucharist miraculously. The readers must decide for themselves about this one.

Here is another pragmatic lesson. Cherish the opportunity to interact with and love the Word of God in writing and Sacrament, but proceed with great caution. God can manage our mistakes, just like a good teaching surgeon can confidently fix any beginner's mistakes, but the way will be longer and more painful.

Another pragmatic lesson - proceed with even more caution as we live with and love those whom God puts in our path, especially our wives, children, grandchildren, nuclear and extended family, his Church, our neighbors locally, and those living in distant lands.

Here's a pragmatic idea for priests to consider. After serving communion, take your time putting away the articles on the altar to give the congregants time to swallow the Eucharist completely before saying, 'Go forth, the Mass is ended,' and expecting them to respond, 'Thanks be to God,' and then to recite the Prayer to Saint Michael the Archangel. Besides,- why rush the kiss between Christ and His Bride?

Perhaps the most poignant lesson for me occurred about two weeks after the incident. I recalled other of Jesus' words, *"I know your works; I know that you are neither cold nor hot. I wish you were either cold or hot. So, because you are lukewarm, neither hot nor cold, I will spit you out of my mouth." (Rev. 3:15-16)* I thought of my sordid past, of the many times I had ignored God's commands and entreaties calling me back to Him. How many times had I spit Jesus out of my mouth? Okay, those sins are forgiven, but how often will I spit Him out of my mouth today?

All these lessons apply to me except for the lesson about not rushing the kiss. And I know God will prompt me to continue searching my soul following this and every other incident in my life to find more, to look for and see Jesus in the myriad events of my life, the myriad mosaic of people, times, and places though, with and in whom He reveals Himself to me. More importantly,

I will look while contemplating what he is trying to teach me in light of the Beatitudes, the Lord's Prayer, and the Sacraments. Who, I must ask myself, other than God, could make this kind of thing up? Who, I must ask myself, can arrange for so many events over so many times and places to fall into their proper order? Who could take the jumbled-up mess I had made of my life and restore order? Who else but God could have straightened the crooked paths I laid down?

Where Will We Look For Jesus?

Where will we, the Church of the twenty-first century, look to find this Jesus who walked the earth in the first century? Will we wrestle with God like Jacob? Will we wrestle with this idea of finding Jesus in the sacraments between the Beatitudes and the Lord's Prayer, a strange and perhaps disturbing idea to ardent Christians who have studied the Bible and worshipped God every Sunday for a lifetime and have given little or no thought to sacraments! Will you ignore the evidence and shrug off the urge to search for Jesus in the sacraments, assuring yourselves that the author of this book sees what he wants to see because he has a sacramental bias?

Granted, you may not believe the lost and found incident. You may find nothing too amazing about how God revealed Himself to me in all of this. I should expect not. Those are my experiences. I can't expect my experiences to move you like they have moved me. But, then again, you do have your experiences.

And so, I ask you, what experiences has God given you to share and contemplate with me? What questions demanding an answer has God asked Protestants and Catholics to share and contemplate together? How many times has Jesus called us to humility? How many times has He called us to worship together? Have there been days when we could have repented more genuinely for having offended God, our neighbor, or each other? How willing are we to meekly depend on God when things are going well, or do we only do that when we struggle?

I ask myself, as well as you. Does our hunger and thirst for justice wane when we enter the sports arenas? Are we more concerned that our team wins, be it football, political, or company brand, than people experiencing poverty receive daily bread? Will we show mercy to the mentally disabled, the sexually addicted, the gender-confused, and other less fortunate people God places in our path, or spend our time railing against invisible, nameless social media foes? Will we be a healing balm for the hurting, the lonely, alienated, hopeless, begging, despondent, and despairing that God places in front of us?

Will we, my Protestant brethren, humbly and courageously explore the truths of God's revelation? Will we meekly depend on God to help us understand each other to share the gospel as one unified holy, apostolic, and I dare say, Catholic Church, even while you may say, "catholic church?

Will we show the world our love for one another so the world can know we are Christians? Will we make Christ and His Church attractive to draw the world to Himself through His Body? Are we willing to suffer, if needed, for the sake of righteousness?

And so, I ask,- where can we find clarity about Jesus' spoken and God's written word? Where can we find Jesus' actions today, demonstrating and confirming His spoken words? Where can we find the written Word with the Word, Himself? Where can we receive Him that is Jesus, the endpoint, not partially as in a concept or as a symbol, but really and completely in His entire person? My answer to these questions is in the Mass. What's your answer?

When we look for and find Jesus in the Mass, we find perfect congruency between His spoken and prayed words in the Sermon on the Mount and His actions in the Church's divine liturgy- this should not surprise us. God's words always match his actions, and what better time than when He, the groom, manifests Himself and His love to His Bride in the perpetual sacrifice of the Mass. This is where the Beatitudes, the Lord's Prayer, and the Sacraments lead us when considering the fourth part of the nine-part analysis. What better way did Jesus have to show love than to give all of himself for His Church once and for all time? What better way does the Church have to receive that love than to receive all of Him, body, soul, humanity, and divinity, thankfully and perpetually without end? I ask again. What's your answer? Will we praise God together with the Angels and all the saints in the Mass?

Finding Jesus

Yes, Christ can change even the hardest and most stubborn among us- I am exhibit A. And yet, more incredible still, by far, is this idea of finding He, who opened the eyes of the blind, created a universe to touch and taste, and raised the dead- finding Him hiding in your spouse, in a grumpy old priest, in material substances like water, oil, and bread, in a little mushy piece of chewed up bread. It sounds shocking and far-fetched, but what if it is true? What if Jesus is Lord of the immaterial and the material universe? I encourage us to contemplate the scriptures, to reread the Sermon on the Mount, and to imagine how it could and, more importantly, should impact our lives.

We must take time to contemplate our lives, our thoughts, words, and actions. We must contemplate God from afar and up close when standing, stooping, squatting, or lying down in all things and all places at all times. Should we lose our way in an operation, a writing exercise, our efforts to love our neighbor or our contemplations, we must ask God and his family for forgiveness and help. They will come to our aid.

For my part, I have decided to continue sharing that little miracle, as you can appreciate, but only within the context of a life well-lived. There would and should be little reason for me to share it with someone I hurt, lied to, cheated, or failed to love as I aught. Why create a scandal for Jesus? I've done enough of that already. On the other hand, if, by God's grace and by His loving presence in my life, I live my remaining days out with integrity, then yes, by all means, I will assuredly proclaim,

what my eyes have seen,
what my hands have touched,
what my tongue has tasted,
and oh yeah, what my ears have heard
and my nose has smelled at Mass when incense is burned.

May this booklet encourage your contemplations, steady your resolve, and draw you closer to Him, who draws all men to God, the Father, Son, and Holy Spirit. Amen!

The Three Side-by-Side

Jesus' Covenant Promise	The Church's Covenant Response	The Holy Exchange of Persons
Blessed are the poor in spirit, for theirs is the kingdom of heaven.	Our Father in heaven,	Baptism – children of God reborn.
Blessed are they who mourn, for they will be comforted	Hallowed be your name,	Confession- children of God reconciled.
Blessed are the meek, for they will inherit the land.	Your kingdom come, your will be done, on earth as in heaven.	Confirmation – children of God re-energized.
Blessed are they who hunger and thirst for righteousness, for they will be satisfied.	Give us today our daily bread;	Eucharist – children of God refueled.
Blessed are the merciful, for they will be shown mercy.	And forgive us our trespasses as we forgive those who trespass against us;	Matrimony – Husband and wife perfectly united with Christ in the center.
Blessed are the clean of heart, for they will see God.	And do not subject us to the final test,	Anointing of the sick –children of God resurrected.

Blessed are the peacemakers, for they will be called children of God.	But deliver us from evil.	Holy Orders –Man a vocation to serve God received.
Blessed are they who are persecuted for the sake of righteousness, for theirs is the kingdom of heaven.	Deliver us, Lord, we pray, from every evil, graciously grant peace in our days, that, by the help of your mercy, we may be always free from sin and safe from all distress, as we await the blessed hope and the coming of our savior, Jesus Christ.	Sacramental economy – the whole salvation plan, Christ empowering the Church to manifest in her liturgy.
Blessed are you when they insult you and persecute you and utter every kind of evil against you [falsely] because of me. Rejoice and be glad, for your reward will be great in heaven. Thus they persecuted the prophets who were before you.	For thine is the kingdom, the power and the glory, now and forever, amen.	The Glorified Christ united with the Church, His Glorified Body manifesting God's will on earth as it is in heaven.

Sermon on the Mount Crossverse Puzzle - version 2

Beatitude	Prayer	Beatitude Clarified	Prayer Clarified	Beatitude/ Prayer Clarified
5:3	6:9a	5:13-16	6:1	6:33
5:4	6:9b	5:17-20	6:2-4	6:34
5:5	6:10	5:21-26	6:5-8	7:1-6
5:6	6:11	5:27-32	6:16-18	7:7-11
5:7	6:12	5:33-37	6:14-15	7:12
5:8	6:13a	5:38-42	6:19-23	7:13-14
5:9	6:13b	5:43-45	6:24	7:15-20
5:10	Embolism	5:46-47	6:25-30	7:21-23
5:11-12	Doxology	5:48	6:31-32	7:24-27

References

- Except for the Lord's Prayer, which is given in the words said in Mass used by the United States Conference of Catholic Bishops (USCCB), all scripture quotations have been taken from New American Bible Revised Edition ("NABRE"). *https://bible.usccb.org/bible*
- Quotes from the Catechism of the Catholic Church (CCC) can be found at: *https://www.usccb.org/sites/default/files/flipbooks/catechism/*

1. A link to the August 7th, 2023 Mass Readings is provided below. *https://bible.usccb.org/bible/readings/080723.cfm*
2. CCC Article 1324, p. 334
3. CCC Article 1076, p. 280
4. Anton Ten Klooster, *Thomas Aquinas On The Beatitudes Reading Matthew, Disputing Grace and Virtue, Preaching Happiness,* Peters Leuven – Paris – Bristol, CT, 2018, pgs. 69-70.
5. Ancient Christian Writers in Translation, vol. 18 *St. Gregory of Nyssa: The Lord's Prayer: The Beatitudes*, translated and annotated by Hilda C. Graef, edited by Johannes Quasten and Joseph C. Plumpe, Paulist Press, p. 130

www.ingramcontent.com/pod-product-compliance
Lightning Source LLC
Chambersburg PA
CBHW070240090526
44586CB00035B/1361